DM

NEW ABSOLUTE APPEAL: DIRECT MAIL DESIGN

ターゲットに効く！ DMデザイン

New Absolute Appeal : Direct Mail Design

PIE International Inc.
4-3-6 Nishigahara, Kita-ku, Tokyo 114-0024 JAPAN
sales@pie-intl.com
©2010 PIE International / PIE BOOKS
ISBN978-4-7562-4016-3
Printed in Japan

CONTENTS

はじめに

NEW
ABSOLUTE
APPEAL:
DIRECT MAIL
DESIGN

ターゲットの手元に直接届けることができる広告メディア、DM。
今、その役割と効果が見直されています。

膨大な情報が溢れるデジタルメディアと異なり、
実際に手に触れることができるDMは、
より強い印象を受け手に残すことができる可能性に溢れています。
また、ある程度ターゲットを絞って届けることができるため、
費用対効果を把握しやすいという利点もあります。

しかし、毎日膨大に郵便受けに届くほかの郵便物との差別化をはかるのは、
容易ではありません。

本書では、ターゲットの心を掴むため、仕掛け・形状・素材にこだわったDMを厳選し、
特集します。
バレエの舞台を再現した立体的な展示会招待状（p.011）や、
紙封筒ではなく真空パックを使用することでブランドイメージを表現したもの（p.033）、
まるで本物の付箋が貼ってあるかのような加工が施されたカタログDM（p.049）、
DMそのものが3Dメガネとなっている展覧会招待状（p.132）など、その手法はさまざま。

それらのDMがどのような戦略によって制作されたのか、
企画・デザインコンセプトもあわせてご紹介します。

企業やブランドが伝えたい価値や商品の魅力を最もダイレクトに伝える手段として、
DMの可能性を感じていただく機会となれば幸いです。

最後になりましたが、本書制作にあたりご多忙な中、多大なご協力を賜りました方々に、
深く御礼を申し上げます。

編集部

FORWARD

NEW
ABSOLUTE
APPEAL:
DIRECT MAIL
DESIGN

The advertising medium, direct mail, delivering its message directly to its audience. Reconsidering its role and its effect.

In contrast to digital media that is packed with a huge volume of information, direct mail that you can actually hold in your hands has the potential to make a greater impact and lasting impression in its recipients.

The fact also that, to a certain degree, they can be sent to a targeted audience means they have the advantage of cost-effectiveness.

However, making direct mail stand out from the huge number of other postal items that arrive in the mailbox every day is not easy.

This book features a range of DMs carefully selected for their unusual approach to devices, shapes and materials used in order to catch the eye of the target audience. Among the featured DMs are a three-dimensional invitation to an exhibition with a reproduction of a ballet stage (page 11); a DM that expresses the brand image using a vacuum pack instead of a paper envelope (page 33); a catalogue DM that has undergone a process to make it look as if real tags are attached (page 49); and an invitation to an exhibition where the DM itself is a pair of 3D glasses (page 132).

Together with their respective planning and design concepts, we also explain the strategy behind the production of the DM.

Here is an opportunity to experience the potential of DM as a means of communicating in the most direct way possible the value or the desirability of a product that a company or brand wishes to communicate.

Finally, we would like to express out heart-felt thanks to all the people who kindly cooperated in the production of this book.

The editors

EDITORIAL NOTE エディトリアルノート

A
カテゴリー
Category

B
デザインコンセプト
Design Concept

C
業種 / 使用目的
Type of Industry / Use Purpose

CL：Client　クライアント
CD：Creative Director　クリエイティブ・ディレクター
AD：Art Director　アート・ディレクター
D：Designer　デザイナー
P：Photographer　カメラマン
I：Illustrator　イラストレーター
CW：Copywriter　コピーライター
DF：Design Firm　制作会社
SB：Submitter　作品提供社

A 010　Apparel

B テーマの世界観を立体的にビジュアル化した
コレクションの招待状

深海に棲む人魚や珊瑚、サーカスでのイメージをテーマにした《DRESS CAMP》2009
年春夏コレクションの招待状。表面上の四面を型抜きすることにより、折り畳まれたときに
球状に就び率になるようなしかけ。中に入っている一枚の紙の裏面に、コレクションの内容を
印刷した。

An invitation to a fashion collection that turned the worldview
of the theme into a three-dimensional visual
An invitation to the 2009 Dress Camp spring/summer collection with a theme consisting of
images of mermaids who dwell in the depths of the sea, prostitutes and circuses. By folding
the invitation, the four surfaces of which had been die cut, it became a three-dimensional
"paper drama." Information on the collection was printed on the back of a sheet of paper
that was inside the invitation.

C アパレル／展示会の招待状　Apparel / Fashion Show Invitation
CL：アパ・・パード KY-ONES　AD、D：K-E Haun　DF、SB：スタッフ・テ Pdyou Co., Ltd

上記以外の制作者呼称は省略せずに掲載しています。
All other production titles are unabbreviated.

本書に掲載されている店名、商品などは、すべて 2010 年 1 月時点での情報になります。
All in store-related information, including shop name, products are accurate as of January 2010.

作品提供者の意向によりデータの一部を記載していない場合があります。
Please note that some credit information has been omitted at the request of the submitter.

各企業名に付随する、〝株式会社、（株）〟および〝有限会社、（有）〟は表記を省略させていただきました。
The 〝kabushiki gaisha (K.K.)〟 and 〝yugen gaisha (Ltd.)〟 portions of all names have been omitted.

本書に記載された企業名・商品名は、掲載各社の商標または登録商標です。
The company and product names that appear in this book are published and/or registered trademarks.

NEW ABSOLUTE APPEAL: DIRECT MAIL DESIGN

ターゲットに効く！ DMデザイン

テーマの世界観を立体的にビジュアル化した
コレクションの招待状

深海に棲む人魚や娼婦、サーカスなどのイメージをテーマとした『DRESS CAMP』2009
年春夏コレクションの招待状。各四方の面を型抜きすることにより、折り畳んだときに立
体的な紙芝居になるよう工夫。中に入っている一枚用紙の裏側に、コレクションの内容を
印刷した。

An invitation to a fashion collection that turned the worldview
of the theme into a three-dimensional visual

An invitation to the 2009 Dress Camp spring/summer collection with a theme consisting of
images of mermaids who dwell in the depths of the sea, prostitutes and circuses. By folding
the invitation, the four surfaces of which had been die cut, it became a three-dimensional
"paper drama." Information on the collection was printed on the back of a sheet of paper
that was inside the invitation.

アパレル / 展示会の招待状   Apparel / Fashion Show Invitation

CL：アト・ワンズ AT ONES'　AD, D：ネスコ Nesco　DF, SB：エヌイグレック Nigrec Co., ltd

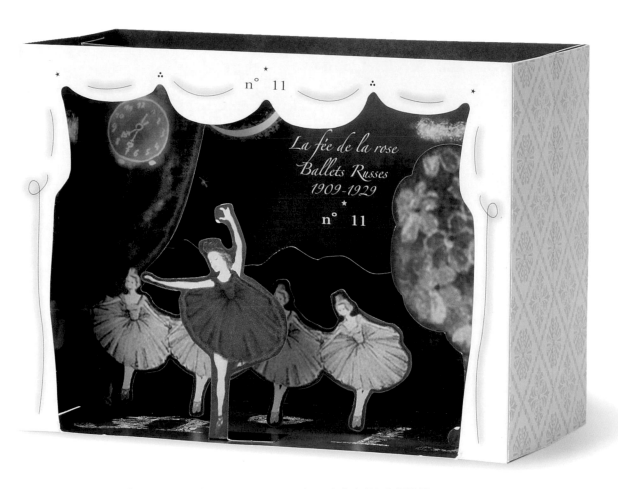

バレエのシーンをモチーフに、エレガントさを表現した招待状

ロシアのバレエ団『Ballets russe（バレエリュス）』にオマージュした『n° 11』の春夏コレクション招待状。バレエの衣装にインスピレーションを得て、オートクチュールのように繊細でエレガントなシリーズを展開。DM ではバレエの舞台を再現し、可憐なイメージを演出した。

An invitation that expresses elegance with a motif of scenes from a ballet

An invitation to the n°11 spring/summer collection that pays homage to the Ballet Russe. Inspired by the costumes of the ballet, an elegant and dainty series was developed in the style of haute couture. The ballet stage was reproduced for the DM to create an engaging image.

アパレル / 展示会の招待状　Apparel / Fashion Show Invitation
CL, SB：シマムラトーキョー・コーポレーション　SHIMAMURA TOKYO CORPORATION

シーズンテーマをシンプルに伝える
コレクションの招待状

『MERRY GO ROUND』をテーマに、白と黒、陰と闇、儚さと繊細さを共存させたニュアンスあるコーディネートを展開する『n° 44』の春夏コレクション招待状。余計な色や要素を排除し、儚くも美しい世界観をストレートに表現した。

An invitation to a fashion collection that conveys a
seasonal theme in a simple way

An invitation to the n°44 spring/summer collection of coordinates featuring nuances of white and black, shadow and darkness, transience and delicacy presented with the theme of a merry-go-round. Extraneous colors and elements were removed and a beautiful yet fleeting worldview was expressed in a direct way.

アパレル / 展示会の招待状
Apparel / Fashion Show Invitation
CL, SB：シマムラトーキョー・コーポレーション　SHIMAMURA TOKYO CORPORATION

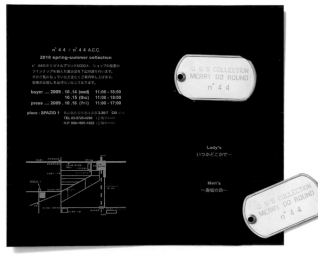

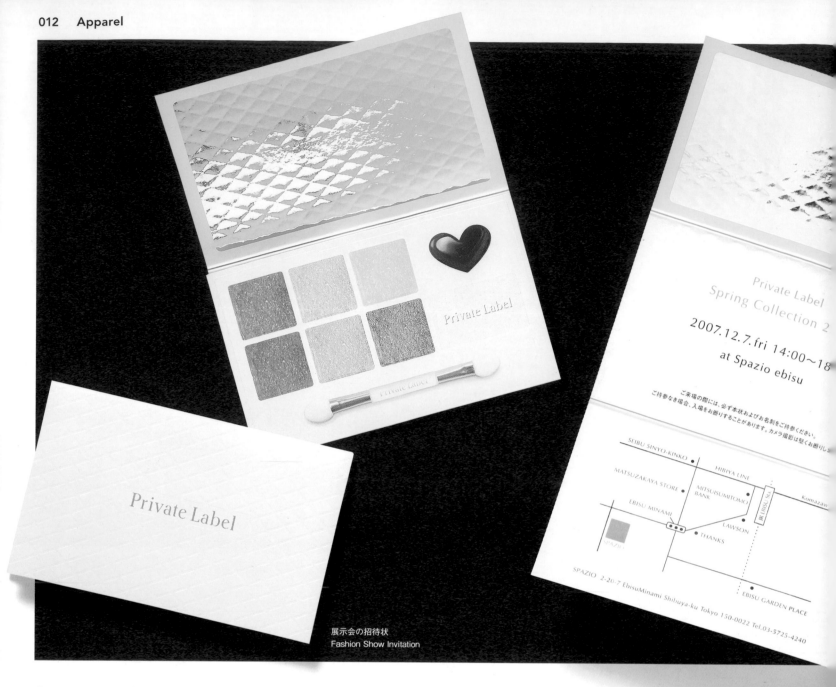

Private Label
Spring Collection 2
2007.12.7.fri 14:00〜18
at Spazio ebisu

ご来場の際には、必ず本状およびお名刺をご持参ください。
ご持参なき場合、入場をお断りすることがあります。カメラ撮影は堅くお断りし

SEIBU SINYO-KINKO
HIBIYA LINE
MATSUZAKAYA STORE
MITSUISUMITOMO BANK
Komazaw
EBISU MINAMI
LAWSON
THANKS
SPAZIO
EBISU GARDEN PLACE
SPAZIO 2-20-7 EbisuMinami Shibuya-ku Tokyo 150-0022 Tel.03-5725-4240

展示会の招待状
Fashion Show Invitation

キュートかつエレガンスな色遣いを駆使したDM

女の子らしさを基調とし、上品で清潔感溢れるカジュアルスタイルを提案する『Private Label』。自分のカラーやスタイルを大
切にするブランドであることから、カラフルで上品な色遣いを意識しながらシーズンコレクションのテーマを表現する。

A DM that maximizes a cute yet elegant color scheme

Private Label, offering an elegant, clean and casual style with a basic feminine tone. The brand holds dear its own colors and style.
The DM therefore expresses the theme of the collection for the season, remaining aware of its colorful yet refined color scheme.

アパレル / 展示会の招待状、季節の挨拶状
Apparel / Fashion Show Invitation, Seasonal Greetings
CL：プライベート レーベル Private Label
D：和田佳子 Yoshiko Wada
DF, SB：プロップ グラフィック ステーション PROP GRAPHIC STATION INC.

展示会の招待状   Fashion Show Invitation

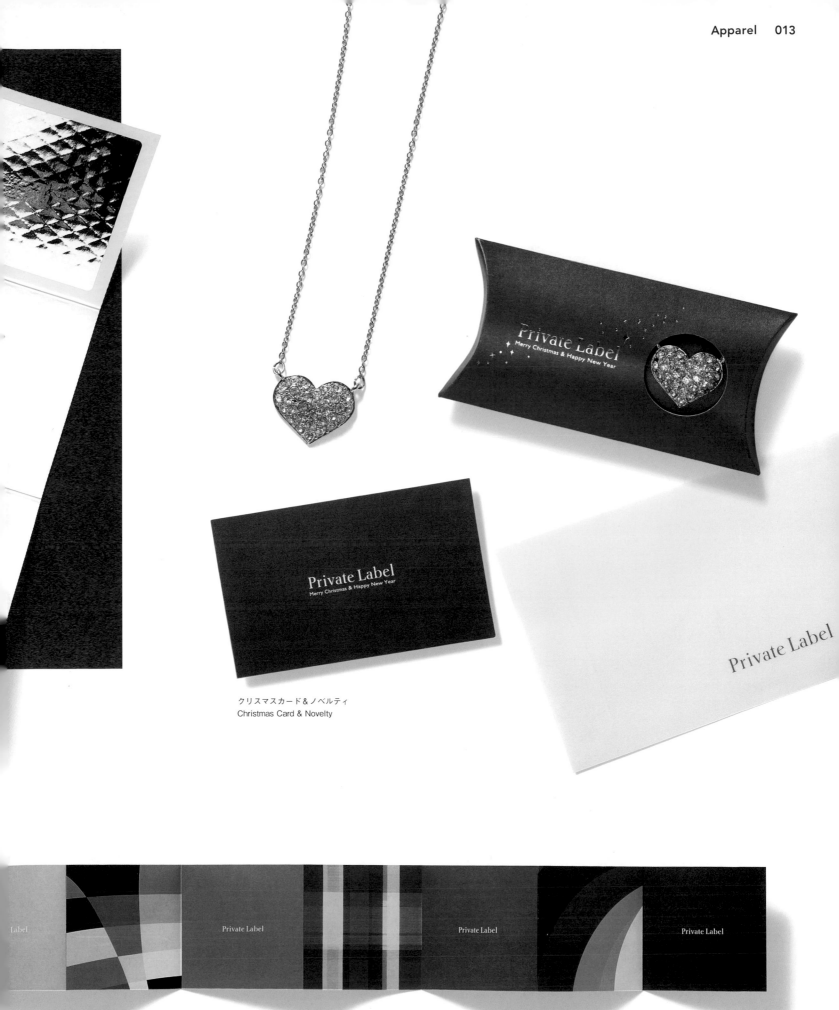

クリスマスカード＆ノベルティ
Christmas Card & Novelty

 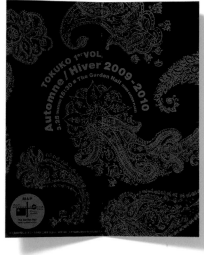 

明快なモチーフとカラフルな色彩で惹きつけるコレクションの招待状

鮮やかな色彩やプリントが魅力のデザイナーズプレタブランド。2009〜2010年秋冬の東京コレクションではロシアを
ディレクションテーマに設定。毎シーズンテーマ国の文化、民族、芸術をデザイン、プリントに表現している。

An invitation to a fashion collection that attracts with a clear motif and a bright color scheme

A designer prêt-a-porter brand with its bright colors and charming prints. For the 2009-2010 autumn/winter Tokyo
collection, the theme was Russia. The culture, people and art of the country that is the season's theme were expressed in the
design and prints.

ファッションブランド / 東京コレクション招待状　Fashion Brand / Collection Invitation

CL：トクコ・プルミエヴォル TOKUKO ler VOL　D：前田徳子 Tokuko Maeda　DF：サティス Satis　SB：レナウン RENOWN INCORPORATED

マダガスカルをディレクションテーマに設定した
コレクションの招待状

マダガスカルをディレクションテーマに設定した2010年春夏コレクションの招待状。多彩なイラストでコレクションの世界観を演出。

An invitation to a fashion collection with a Madagascar theme

An invitation to the 2010 spring/summer fashion collection with an inderlying theme of Madagascar. The collection's worldview is produced using various illustrations.

ファッションブランド / 東京コレクション招待状
Fashion Brand / Collection Invitation
CL：トクコ・プルミエヴォル TOKUKO ler VOL　D：前田徳子 Tokuko Maeda
DF：サティス Satis　SB：レナウン RENOWN INCORPORATED

コレクションのテーマをPOPに表現した
展示会の招待状

2008年秋冬コレクションの展示会招待状。『LOVE ROCK』というコンセプトのもと、ガーリーな中にロックテイストをミックスし、少しレトロで刺激的なファッションを展開。DMもレトロなレコードをモチーフにし、星マークを多用してROCKな気分が高まるデザインに。

An invitation to an exhibition with a pop expression of the theme of the collection

An invitation to the 2008 autumn/winter collection. Based on the concept of LOVE ROCK, an exciting fashion range that was slightly retro mixed with touches of girly and rock chic was presented. The DM also had a motif of an old-style record and the star mark was widely used for the design to produce even more of a rock look.

アパレル / 展示会の招待状
Apparel / Fashion Show Invitation
CL：ジョリーブティック Jolly Boutique, INC.
D：和田佳子 Yoshiko Wada
DF, SB：プロップ グラフィック ステーション PROP GRAPHIC STATION INC.

ブランドにまつわるアイテムで構成したパーティの案内状

2008年秋冬メンズプレタポルテ・コレクションショーのパーティ案内状。ベーシックな紺色をベースに、ブランドにまつわる様々なアイテムで構成。なかでも、頭文字の『H』、ブランドの象徴である馬具、年間テーマの『眩惑のインド』から連想したゾウを抜粋、コースター仕様のカードを制作し同封した。

Party information using items surrounding the brand

Party information for the 2008 autumn/winter men's prêt-a-porter collection show. With a base of basic dark blue, the information consists of items associated with the brand. The letter H, the harness that symbolizes the brand and the elephant that is part of the season's theme were extracted and turned into coaster-style cards that were then enclosed.

アパレル / パーティの案内状   Apparel / Party Invitation
CL：エルメスジャポン　HERMÈS JAPON　AD, D, SB：グルーヴィジョンズ　groovisions

新作バッグそのものをモチーフにしたDM

エルメスの日本限定モデル『ビュールサングル』のDM＆フライヤー。カジュアル感と気品を兼ね備えた新作バッグの、淡くカラフルな色遣いやなめらかなエッジをイラストでアイコン化し、DMの窓からのぞかせて楽しさを演出した。バッグの形をしたフライヤーは店頭で配布。統一したビジュアルでより強い印象付けを狙った。

DM with new-release bags as a motif

DM and leaflet for the Hermès Pursangle, available only in Japan. The light yet bright color scheme and the smooth edges of this "smart-casual" new bag have been turned into icons using illustration to produce a sense of fun as they peek through the window in the DM. The bag-shaped leaflet was distributed in store. The aim was to create a more powerful impression with consistent visuals.

アパレル / 新商品の案内状
Apparel / New Merchandise Announcement
CL：エルメスジャポン　HERMÈS JAPON
AD, D, SB：グルーヴィジョンズ　groovisions

上質感のある煌びやかさを演出した
クリスマス・パーティの招待状

シックな紺色とシルバーで上品な華やかさを演出。招待状はクリスマスプレゼントの箱を象り、ブランドやシーズンテーマを象徴するアイテムを散らばらせた。

A Christmas party invitation with a high-quality dazzling effect

An elegant gorgeousness produced with a chic dark blue and silver. The invitation resembles a box containing a Christmas present and is covered in items that symbolize the brand and the season's theme.

アパレル / パーティの案内状
Apparel / Party Invitation
CL：エルメスジャポン　HERMÈS JAPON
AD, D, SB：グルーヴィジョンズ　groovisions

NOËL DE FRANCE

本年もエルメスをご愛顧いただきましてありがとうございました。
この一年の感謝の気持ちを込めて、下記の通りクリスマス・パーティを開催いたします。
『ノエル・ド・フランス』をみなさまとお祝いしたく、ご来店のほどスタッフ一同よりお待ちしております。

エルメス藤崎店

日時：2008年11月16日（日）午後1時〜午後7時

お問合せ先：022-261-5111
ご来場の際は本状をお持ちください。
当日はシャンパンをご用意しておりますので、お車でのご来場はご遠慮くださいますようお願いいたします。

Venez découvrir le nouveau sac
Pursangle
chez Hermès Midosuji

エルメス御堂筋店は、特別に日本限定の新作バッグ、ピュールサングルを
先行してご紹介いたします。みなさまのご来店を心よりお待ち申し上げます。

2009年4月8日（水）から
4月25日（土）より一般発売

エルメス御堂筋店　お問合せ先：06-4704-7110

コレクションの妖艶なイメージを表現した招待状

『DRESS CAMP』2009年秋冬コレクションの招待状。ゴシックや娼婦などといった独特のモチーフがテーマ。和のイメージもあったため、形を屏風形式に。3枚合紙を蛇腹折りの仕様にし、箔押しをしたスリーブのケースを付けた。

An invitation that expresses the bewitching image of the collection

An invitation to the 2009 autumn/winter DRESS CAMP collection. The theme is unique motifs such as Gothic and prostitute. As the collection also has a Japanese image, shapes were created in the form of folding screens. Three sheets of paper were joined together into an accordion fold and contained a sleeve covered in foil.

アパレル / 展示会の招待状
Apparel / Fashion Show Invitation
CL：アト・ワンズ AT ONES' AD, D：ネスコ Nesco DF, SB：エヌイグレック Nigrec Co., ltd

ブランドコンセプトやトレンドをストレートに伝える案内状

『Precious, but easy』を掲げ、ファッション感度の高い女性に向けて、贅沢さと楽しさを共存させたオリジナルアイテムを発信するショップ『FRANQUEENSENSE』のプレスプレビュー案内状。ブランドコンセプトにマッチした紙や印刷手法を選び、ヒップでスタイリッシュな世界観を演出する。

Information that conveys the brand concept and trends in a direct way

A press preview notice for the shop FRANQUEENSENSE offering original items that are both luxurious and fun for fashion-conscious women based on a "Precious, but easy" idea. The paper and the printing technique were chosen to match the brand concept and produce a stylish and hip worldview.

アパレル / プレスプレビューの案内状
Apparel / Press Preview Announcement
CL：ペレニアル ユナイテッドアローズ　PERENNIAL UNITED ARROWS Ltd.　CD, AD：横枕芳美　Yoshimi Yokomakura
D：小池晴子　Haruko Koike　P (2009ss)：菅原有希子　Yukiko Sugawara
DF, SB：プロップ グラフィック ステーション　PROP GRAPHIC STATION INC.

ポスターとDMを兼務させ、展開時の画面構成を工夫したコンペ告知

オリジナルニットキャップのデザインフェスティバル『KNIT CAP CUP』の告知DM。ポスターとDM
を分けて制作するという依頼だったが、折りを工夫して、両方兼務するつくりを提案。折っているとき
と開いたときの展開の違いを楽しめるよう、画面構成を計算した。

A joint poster and DM announcing a competition with a cleverly developed composition

A DM announcing the original knit cap design festival, KNIT CAP CUP. The brief was to produce the
poster and the DM separately, but it was suggested that the same design could be used for both by
manipulating the folds. The picture-plane composition was calculated so that fun could be had with the
differences between the folded and unfolded version.

ニットメーカー / コンペ告知DM　Knit Manufacturer / Festival Announcement
CL：白倉ニット　SHIRAKURA KNIT CO., LTD.　AD, D, I：紀太みどり　Midori Kida　P：佐原理枝　Rie Sahara
CD：春蒔プロジェクト　Harumaki Project co., ltd.　DF, SB：タイニー　tiny

『大人可愛い世界観』を表現した展示会の招待状

黒と燻したような金色でまとめ、ポイントで使用しているリボンには『贈り物』という気持ちを込めた。トルソーのシルエットで遊び心も演出。

An invitation to an exhibition that expresses a "grown-up cute" worldview

The design of the invitation was brought together with black and a smoky gold and the ribbon that was used contained the message of "present." A sense of fun was produced with a silhouette of the torso.

アパレル / 展示会の招待状
Apparel / Fashion Show Invitation
CL：グラン山貴 Gran Yamaki Inc.　DF, SB：セルディビジョン CELL DIVISION

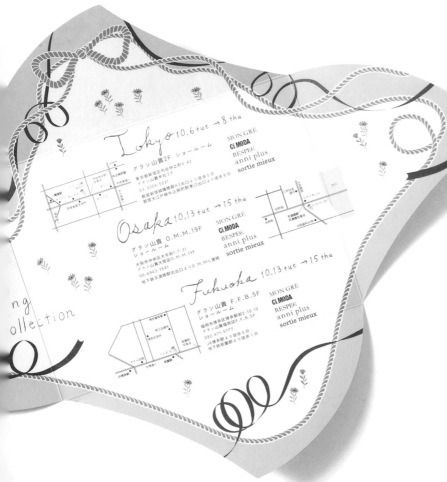

春風をイメージさせる
ハンカチをモチーフにした展示会の招待状

春のコレクション展示会の招待状。封を開けると風に舞うハンカチのように見えるデザインにし、軽やかで心躍るようなコレクションのイメージを表現した。

Exhibition invitiation with a motif of a handkerchief and a spring breeze

An invitation to an exhibition of the spring collection. The invitation was designed to look like a handkerchief dancing in the wind when the seal is opened, expressing the light "dancing heart" image of the collection.

アパレル / 展示会の招待状
Apparel / Fashion Show Invitation
CL：グラン山貴　Gran Yamaki Inc.
DF, SB：セルディビジョン CELL DIVISION

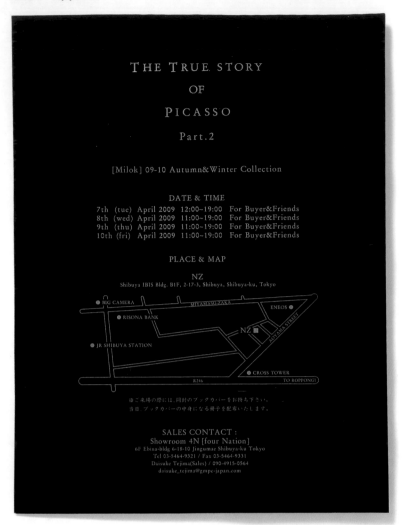

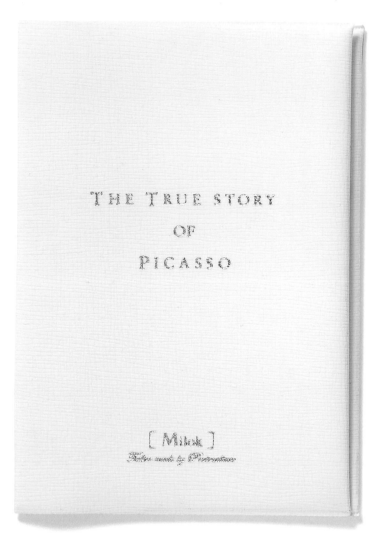

黒と白のブックカバーを同封したコレクションの招待状

『Milok』2009年秋冬コレクションの招待状。展示会で配る小冊子のブックカバーを同封。封筒にはミラーコートとトレペを使用し、ブックカバーはPVCに箔押しを施した。第1弾と第2弾を展開。第2弾は、黒の封筒に白のブックカバーで色を変えている。

An invitation to a fashion show with a black and white book cover enclosed

An invitation to the 2009 autumn/winter Milok collection with a book cover for the pamphlet distributed at the show enclosed. Mirrorkote and tracing paper were used for the envelope and PVC and foil for the book cover. Two versions were created. The color was changed for the second version to a black envelope and white book cover.

アパレル／展示会の招待状　　Apparel / Fashion Show Invitation

CL：LDK100 LDK100 Co., Ltd　AD, D：ネスコ Nesco　DF, SB：エヌイグレック Nigrec Co., ltd

石盤をイメージして制作したコレクションの招待状

『石盤を送りつける』をコンセプトとした『Motel』2009年秋冬コレクションの招待状。型押しのエンボス加工、エンボスの紙、石のテクスチャ印刷の3トップで石のイメージに近づけた。中を開けて欲しくないDMだが、万が一開けた人のために、『YES WE CAN』を印刷した用紙を同封。

An invitation to a fashion collection with an image of a writing slate

An invitation to the 2009 autumn/winter Motel collection with its concept of "sending a writing slate." The look of the stone was created with a combination of stamp embossing, embossed paper and printing the texture of the stone. The DM was not designed to be opened out but if someone were to do so, inside is enclosed a sheet of paper containing the words "Yes, we can".

アパレル / 展示会の招待状   Apparel / Fashion Show Invitation

CL：モーテル MOTEL inc.   AD, D：ネスコ Nesco   DF, SB：エヌイグレック Nigrec Co., ltd

星座早見盤をモチーフにした展示会の招待状

ファッションブランドMOSSLIGHTの展示会『AW 2006-07
MOSSLIGHT EXHIBITION』は星座をシーズンテーマに開催。
その世界観を星座早見盤の形態で案内状を制作し表現。レコード
のEP盤のサイズにし、ジャケットに収納できるようにした。

**An invitation to a fashion collection with a
constellation chart motif**

The season's theme for the 2006-07 Autumn/Winter Mosslight
fashion brand's show was constellations. The brand's worldview
was expressed by turning the event information into a constellation
chart. It was the same size as an EP record and designed to be
inserted into a record sleeve.

ファッションブランド / イベントの告知、展示会の招待状
Fashion Brand / Event Announcement, Fashion Show Invitation
CL：モスライト MOSSLIGHT　AD, D, SB：エンライトメント Enlightenment

∞

AW 2006-07 MOSSLIGHT EXHIBITION
Daily life of Mikrokosmos

MOSSLIGHT PRESS / 4F Nishiazabu 28 mori Bldg. 4-16-13 Nishiazabu minato-ku Tokyo Japan 106-8629
Phone : 81 3 5469 6302   info@mosslight.net

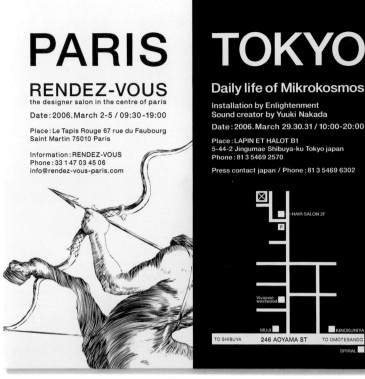

PARIS
RENDEZ-VOUS
the designer salon in the centre of paris

Date : 2006. March 2-5 / 09:30-19:00

Place : Le Tapis Rouge 67 rue du Faubourg
Saint Martin 75010 Paris

Information : RENDEZ-VOUS
Phone : 33 1 47 03 45 06
info@rendez-vous-paris.com

TOKYO
Daily life of Mikrokosmos

Installation by Enlightenment
Sound creator by Yuuki Nakada

Date : 2006. March 29.30.31 / 10:00-20:00

Place : LAPIN ET HALOT B1
5-44-2 Jingumae Shibuya-ku Tokyo japan
Phone : 81 3 5469 2570

Press contact japan / Phone : 81 3 5469 6302

246 AOYAMA ST

∞
MOSSLIGHT

Secret Venus

There is a secret of Venus of Milo.

When I was a child, I asked my mother why the sculpture has no arms.
The armless body of the Venus has given us all kinds of imaginations.
Was she taking her dress off? Or was she holding a knife as a weapon?
Or had she ever never had any arms?

Nowadays, it is not necessary to grope our ways and we are tied down with
all sorts of overflowing information.
I cannot stop feeling that the Venus of Milo is smiling cynically at us.
What is the charm of incompleteness? It shakes our concealed inquiring mind
and gives us hopes and whole new world to discover.

We create an infinite alternative couture fashion that has the charm of incompleteness
yet still of which we can wear in our everyday life.

RENDEZ-VOUS the new designer salon in the centre of paris
DATE / 2005. October 6,7,8 - 10h-19h
PLACE / Espace Pierre Cardin 1-3 avenue Gabriel 75008 paris
METRO / Concorde

Information / RENDEZ-VOUS : 144 rue de Rivoli, 75001 PARIS
T (+33) 1 47 03 45 06, F (+33) 1 49 027 04 58, info@rendez-vous-paris.com

Contact with us / MOSSLIGHT [Yasutaka Tomita, Michiko Nakayama]
T (+81) 90 65 45 58 81, info@mosslight.net
From 2-13 oct, communicate in paris
Mobile (+81) 90 65 45 58 81, Fax 01 43 87 03 29, info@mosslight.net

VIDEO INSTALLATION / Enlightenment

独自のデザイン世界を広げる
ファッションブランドの招待状

『S/S 2006 MOSSLIGHT INSTALLATION』の招待状。斤量のある厚紙に、油絵タッチのフクロウの絵を印刷。封筒にはシルエットのフクロウが抜けている。

An invitation to a collection for a fashion brand enlarging its unique design world
An invitation to the 2006 spring/summer MOSSLIGHT INSTALLATION collection. An oil painting-style image of an owl was printed on heavy cardboard. The envelope contains the owl in silhouette.

ファッションブランド / イベントの告知、展示会の招待状
Fashion Brand / Event Announcement, Fashion Show Invitation
CL：モスライト MOSSLIGHT   AD, D, SB：エンライトメント Enlightenment

楽譜をリアルにデザインし、テーマをストレートに伝えた招待状

『Y's』2009年秋冬コレクションの招待状。『sing a song』がテーマであるため、子供のときに使った譜面を
モチーフにデザイン。カバーは色上質紙を使い、無線綴じにした。

An invitation with a realistic design of a musical score to convey the theme in a direct way

An invitation to Y's autumn/winter 2009 collection. As the theme is "sing a song," the design contains a motif of a sheet of music used by young children. High-quality colored paper was used for the cover and the invitation was perfect-bound.

アパレル / 展示会の招待状
Apparel / Fashion Show Invitation

CL：ヨウジヤマモト Yohji Yamamoto inc.   AD, D：ネスコ Nesco   DF, SB：エヌイグレック Nigrec Co., ltd

ブランドイメージを伝え、インパクトを狙った展示会の招待状

『KATHARINE HAMNETT』『HAMNETT』『MORGAN HOMME』といった個性的なインターナショナルブランドを展開する『OHGA』のシーズンコレクション招待状。アバンギャルドでセクシーなブランドイメージをストレートに表現し、勢いとインパクトのあるDMに仕立てた。

An invitation to a fashion collection that aims to make an impact in conveying the brand image

An invitation to the OHGA season collection presented by the unique international brands, KATHARINE HAMNETT, HAMNETT and MORGAN HOMME. The avant-garde, sexy brand image was expressed in a direct way to create a DM that had force and impact.

アパレル / 展示会の招待状 Apparel / Fashion Show Invitation
CL：大賀 OHGA.CO., LTD. D：和田佳子 Yoshiko Wada DF, SB：プロップ グラフィック ステーション PROP GRAPHIC STATION INC.
Agency：コスモ・コミュニケーションズ Cosmo Communications Inc.

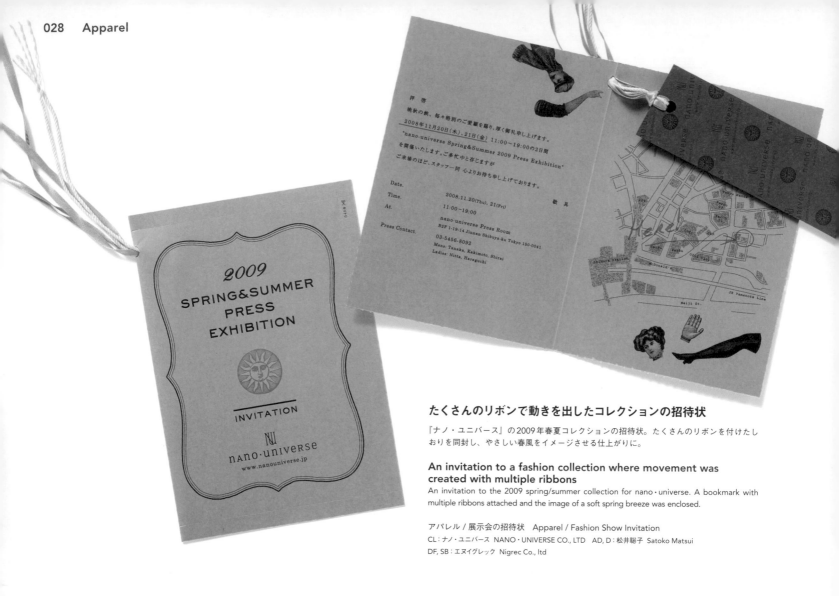

たくさんのリボンで動きを出したコレクションの招待状

『ナノ・ユニバース』の2009年春夏コレクションの招待状。たくさんのリボンを付けたしおりを同封し、やさしい春風をイメージさせる仕上がりに。

An invitation to a fashion collection where movement was created with multiple ribbons

An invitation to the 2009 spring/summer collection for nano・universe. A bookmark with multiple ribbons attached and the image of a soft spring breeze was enclosed.

アパレル / 展示会の招待状　Apparel / Fashion Show Invitation
CL：ナノ・ユニバース　NANO・UNIVERSE CO., LTD　AD, D：松井聡子　Satoko Matsui
DF, SB：エヌイグレック　Nigrec Co., ltd

クチュールの優雅な雰囲気を
イメージさせる招待状

『ナノ・ユニバース』の2009年秋冬コレクションの招待状。テーマが『Daily Couture』であるため、ロマンティックで上質な時間を連想させるDMを制作した。

An invitation containing the elegant ambience of couture

An invitation to the 2009 autumn/winter collection of nano・universe. As the theme was "daily couture," the DM produced suggested romantic high-quality time.

アパレル / 展示会の招待状
Apparel / Fashion Show Invitation
CL：ナノ・ユニバース　NANO・UNIVERSE CO., LTD
AD, D：松井聡子　Satoko Matsui　DF, SB：エヌイグレック　Nigrec Co., ltd

Exhibition Schedule:

For Buyer
20th (tue) October 14:00~20:00
21st (wed) October 10:00~20:00
22nd (thu) October 10:00~20:00

For Press & Friends
22nd (thu) October 11:00~20:00
23rd (fri) October 11:00~20:00

＊Please make an appointment prior to your arrival.

G.B.7

Invitation
2010 Spring & Summer
Collection

3 : Contact Information

Open Here ↓

Place & Map :
ASSEMBLY ROOM 632-A
2F Bakery Café 632, 6-32-10, Jingumae,
Shibuya-ku, Tokyo, 151-0001, Japan.

何通もDMが届いた演出をし、
展示会への期待感を高めた招待状

『Motel』2010年春夏コレクションの招待状。『一度に何種類もの
DMを届けたい！』がデザインコンセプト。それぞれの封筒がくっ
ついたトリックデザインで、各封筒を開くと展示会情報が記載され
ている。

**An invitation consisting of multiple DMs to
raise the sense of anticipation for a fashion
event**

An invitation to the 2010 spring/summer Motel collection. The
design concept was to send multiple DMs at one time. A "trick"
design where the envelope that is attached to each DM contains
information on the event.

アパレル／展示会の招待状
Apparel / Fashion Show Invitation
CL：モーテル MOTEL inc.   AD, D：ネスコ Nesco
DF, SB：エヌイグレック Nigrec Co., ltd

ラメ入りの紙で、さりげない豪華さを演出した展示会の招待状

『gomme GOMME HOMME』の展示会の招待状。誕生20周年のスペシャル感を出すために、普段より少し豪華な仕様に。ラメ入りのスペシャリティーズNo.903を使い、一見、黒に見えるが、よく見るとラメ入りの紙で作ったパズルになっているというさりげない演出で豪華さを表現した。

Casual magnificence using lamé paper for an invitation to a fashion show

An invitation to the gomme GOMME HOMME fashion show. To create a sense of the special nature of the 20th anniversary, the design specifications were slightly more luxurious than usual. Gorgeousness was expressed in a casual way with a puzzle made using lamé paper No. 903 Specialized, which at first glance appears to be black but when examined more closely contains gold lamé.

アパレル / 展示会の招待状　Apparel / Fashion Show Invitation
CL：マキヒロシゲアトリエ　MAKI HIROSHIGE ATELIER CO., LTD.　AD, D：鷲見 陽　Akira Sumi
DF, SB：アンテナグラフィックベース　Antenna Graphic Base CO., LTD.

素材の質感を効果的に魅せたパリコレの招待状

2009年秋冬コレクションは、独特な『革』の雰囲気とパリコレ会場である『パレ・ド・トウキョウ』のイメージをミックスした。

An invitation to view the Paris collection enhanced to good effect with the texture of the fabrics

The 2009 Autumn/Winter collection combines a unique atmosphere of leather and an image of Paris de Tokio that is the venue for the Paris collection.

アパレル / パリコレ招待状
Apparel / Invitation to View the Paris Collection
CL：エー.ティー.ディー.エス　A.T.D.S INC. / アツロウ タヤマ　ATSURO TAYAMA
D：吉田望絵　Moe Yoshida
DF, SB：プロップ グラフィック ステーション　PROP GRAPHIC STATION INC.

ビジュアルや質感にアクセントをつけた新商品の案内

洗練された大人の着こなしを提案するAdam et Ropéが掲げたシーズンテーマは『PUNK COUTURE』。三つ折りからのぞくモデル写真のビジュアルアクセントや、質感につけたギャップ等から、同ブランドによる『反抗→既成概念からの自由』を感じられるようにした。

New product announcement with accents of visuals and textures

The season's theme for Adam et Ropé that offers stylish, refined dressing was "Punk Couture." From the visual accent consisting of photographs of models that can be spied through the tri-fold format and gaps applied to create textures etc, the brand's concept "Resistance is freedom from accepted ideas" was conveyed.

アパレル / 新商品の案内状　Apparel / New Merchandise Announcement
CL：ジュン JUN Co., Ltd.　AD, D, SB：浜田武士 Takeshi Hamada
P：ハスイモトヒコ (FEMME) Motohiko Hasui (FEMME)
Hair：松本和也 (FEMME) Kazuya Matsumoto (FEMME)　Make-up：Akii

コレクションのテーマを活かした展示会の招待状

様々なブランドとのコラボレーションを行うラグジュアリー・スポーツ・ウェア『ハイドロゲン』の展示会招待状。自動車と関連のあるコレクションであったため、封筒をメタリックなものに。中のカードは『ワッペン』をキーワードにデザインした。

Invitation to an exhibition that maximizes the theme of the collection

An invitation to an exhibition of the luxury sportswear brand Hydrogen. As the collection was related to motor vehicles, the envelope was metallic. The card inside was designed with the keyword of "coat of arms".

アパレル / 展示会の招待状　Apparel / Fashion Show Invitation
CL：三喜商事 SANKI SHOJI CO., LTD. / ハイドロゲン HYDROGEN　D：吉田望絵 Moe Yoshida
DF, SB：プロップ グラフィック ステーション PROP GRAPHIC STATION INC.

ALL UNDERGROUND DUDES
2009 A/W EXHIBITION
3/24/THU-27/FRI/2009
Mod of Rag
10:00AM-19:00PM/AT SPACE EDGE

DVDのパッケージを招待状にしたファッションブランドのDM

モードの要素（パタン、縫製技術など）とストリートの要素（男らしさ、実用性など）の融合をブランドコンセプトとするMod of Rag。ブランド紹介のDVDを招待状を兼ねたパッケージで包装し送付することで、印象深く、いつまでもとっておいてもらえるようなDMを狙った。

Fashion brand DM with a DVD package turned into an invitation

Mod of Rag, with its brand concept that is a fusion of fashion elements (patterns, sewing techniques) and street elements (masculinity, practicality). The DVD that introduces the brand was sent out wrapped in packaging that also serves as an invitation with the aim of creating an impressive DM that would be kept forever.

アパレル、メンズファッションブランド / 展示会の招待状
Apparel, Men's Fashion Brand / Fashion Show Invitation
CL：モッドオブラグ　Mod of Rag　Art Work, SB：西舘朋央　Tomoo Nishidate
D：川島卓也　Takuya Kawashima

腑分図 09/10

DEVOA

Anatomical Chart 09/10
DEVOA 2009-10 A/W Exhibition

FOR BUYER
17 Tue. — 19 Thu. February 2009
10am—7pm (19 Thu. 10am—5pm)

FOR PRESS & FRIENDS
20 Fri. February 2009 10am—5pm

DEVOA SHOWROOM
2-24-14 Meguro-honcho
Meguro-ku Tokyo 152-0002 Japan
Phone: +81(0)3 57 68 52 11

TOKYU BUS 黒01 (To Ookayama Elementary School)
Meguro Station — Himonya 2chome

OFFICE
2-24-14 Meguro-honcho
Meguro-ku Tokyo 152-0002 Japan
Phone: +81(0)3 57 68 52 11
Facsimile: +81(0)3 57 68 52 12
E-mail: info@devoa.jp
www.devoa.jp

ネパールの手漉き紙を使用した展示会の招待状

レスリング出身で、スポーツ医学や人体力学などを学んだ異色の経歴を持つデザイナー西田大介氏によるメンズファッションブランド。人体を知り尽くした西田氏の立体的かつ斬新な作品を体現できるデザインを目指した。ロクタ紙（ネパールの手漉き紙）に金箔押しし真空パックすることでブランドイメージを表現。

Handmade paper from Nepal for an invitation to an exhibition

A men's fashion brand by designer Daisuke Nishida who has had a unique career that includes wrestling, sports medicine and body mechanics. The aim of the design was to personify the three-dimensional and innovative work of Nishida who knows the human body through and through. The brand image was expressed by applying gold foil to the Nepalese handmade paper of the invitation and vacuum packing.

アパレル / 展示会の招待状　Apparel / Fashion Show Invitation
CL：DEVOA　AD, D：大原健一郎　Kenichiro Ohara　DF, SB：ナイン　NIGN co., Ltd.

展示会のテーマ『さなぎ』を連想させる招待状

知的で繊細なディテールと、マテリアル使いを得意とするデザイナー岡庭智明氏によるメンズファッションブランド。ロウ引き後の封筒を1枚1枚手でしわ加工し3層重ねにすることで、展示会のテーマである『さなぎ』を連想できるようなDMを制作。

An association with the theme of "pupa" for an invitation to an exhibition

A men's fashion brand by designer Tomoaki Okaniwa known for his clever and delicate detailing and use of materials. Each of the waxed envelopes underwent a creasing process and then formed into layers of three to make an association with the theme of the exhibition of "pupa."

アパレル / 展示会の招待状　Apparel / Fashion Show Invitation
CL：キャタピラープロデュイ　Caterpillar Produit Co., Ltd.
AD, D：大原健一郎　Kenichiro Ohara　DF, SB：ナイン　NIGN co., Ltd.

フワフワ・キラキラの素材を用いたクリスマス＆新年の挨拶状

ソフトな感触で高級感のある『ヴィベール』と光沢紙『シャインフェイス』の合紙を使用。
温かくてリッチな素材感を大切にデザインした。

A Christmas and New Year greeting card using soft and sparkly materials

A combination of the soft-to-the-touch, high-quality Vivelle paper and the shiny Shineface paper was
used. The design emphasized the warm, rich texture of the materials.

アパレル / 季節の挨拶状
Apparel / Seasonal Greetings
CL：サンエーインターナショナル　SANEI INTERNATIONAL　D：小池晴子　Haruko Koike
DF, SB：プロップ グラフィック ステーション　PROP GRAPHIC STATION INC.

ブランドイメージを大切に届けるセール案内

ブリティッシュ・スタイルを意識しながら、斬新さと完成度にこだわった流行に左右されない男服を展開し続ける『メンズ・ビギ』。セール案内の
DMもブランドイメージに合わせ、男性的かつ高級感を表現した。

Sale announcement that cherishes the brand image

The classic men's fashion label, Men's Bigi, which emphasizes innovation and a high degree of finish while incorporating a sense of British style. To align
with the brand image, masculinity and high quality were expressed in the sale information DM too.

アパレル / セールの案内状　Apparel / Sale Information
CL：メンズ・ビギ　MENS' BIGI CO., LTD.　AD, D：鷲見 陽　Akira Sumi　D：澤田千尋　Chihiro Sawada　DF, SB：アンテナグラフィックベース　Antenna Graphic Base CO., LTD.

温もりを出すため、紙や印刷の質感に こだわったクリスマスカード

『手触り感のあるクリスマスカードを作りたい』というクライアントのコンセプトから、紙や印刷手法、サイズにこだわった。『桃はだ』という紙に、シルバーとブルーメタル箔を使用。クリスマス感を出しつつ、温かみや可愛らしさを表現した。

A Christmas card where particular consideration was paid to the texture of the paper and the printing

As the client's concept was to create a Christmas card with a tactile element, particular consideration was paid to the paper, the printing technique and the size of the card. Silver and blue metal foil was used on paper called Momohada. To create a Christmas atmosphere, a sense of warmth and loveliness were expressed.

アパレル / 季節の挨拶状　Apparel / Seasonal Greetings
CL：スマイル　Smile inc.　Logo Design：Alex Wiederin
D：小池晴子　Haruko Koike
DF, SB：プロップ グラフィック ステーション　PROP GRAPHIC STATION INC.

有機物でシュールな世界観を展開する
コレクションの招待状

有機物の持つ生々しさと美しさを合わせたシュールな世界観を表現。タイトルロゴ
にも有機的な要素を加え、どことなくミステリアスな印象を持たせるものとした。
封筒は、インパクトのある作品ビジュアルのみが印刷されたデザインに。

An invitation to a collection that presents a surreal worldview using organic matter

A surreal worldview that matched the freshness and the beauty of organic matter
was expressed. Organic elements were added to the title logo to add a vague sense
of mystery. The envelope was printed only with the powerful visuals.

アパレル / 展示会の招待状
Apparel / Fashion Show Invitation
CL：アーモンド・アイ ALMOND EYE CO., LTD   DF, SB：セルディビジョン CELL DIVISION

テーマの『リサイクル』を
様々な形で反映させた展示会の招待状

『RITSUKO SHIRAHAMA』のコレクション展示会の招待状。
テーマが『リサイクル』であるため、ブランド名の頭文字とリ
サイクルの『R』をモチーフに切り抜き、通常捨てられる部分
をショーの引き換え券として利用。生地パターンの落ち葉画像
を地球に見立て、ゴミ箱の形とリンクさせて、環境問題を提起
している。

An invitation to an exhibition that reflects in various forms the theme of recycling

An invitation to the exhibition of the Ritsuko Shirahama
collection. As the theme was recycling, die-cuts were
made of the first letter in the brand name and the R in recycling
to be the motif and the parts that are generally thrown
away were used as exchange coupons for the show. The
image of fallen leaves in the patterns on the fabric were
made to resemble the earth and environmental issues were
raised by linking with the shape of a rubbish tin.

アパレル / 展示会の招待状
Apparel / Fashion Show Invitation
CL：アーモンド・アイ ALMOND EYE CO., LTD
DF, SB：セルディビジョン CELL DIVISION

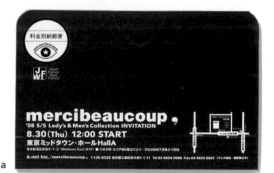

a

b

シーズンテーマの楽しさを伝えるコレクション招待状

『きちんとしているけれど、ちょっと笑える。主張はあるけど、気どっていない。』をテーマとしたファッションブランド。2008年S/S (a) は、シーズン・テーマ『星』にもとづき、『みんな見てるし、見られてる』というメッセージを込め、星形のメガネをモチーフとしたDMに、2008年A/W (b) は、シーズン・テーマ『コミュニケーション』から、文字を使ったパッケージにした。2007年S/S (c) は『見えない敵との戦い』というテーマから架空のフルーツ・モンスターのトレーディング・カードをモチーフに、2007年A/Wは『つながり』というテーマからパズルをモチーフにデザインした。

Conveying the fun of the season's theme for an invitation to a fashion collection
A fashion brand whose theme is "I take things seriously but I can laugh a little too. I have opinions but I'm not pretentious." The season theme for the 2008 spring/summer collection (a) was "stars." The DM had a motif of star-shaped eye glasses that incorporated the message "Everyone's watching, everyone's being watched." From the season's theme for the 2008 autumn/winter collection (b) of "communication," the DM was turned into typographic packaging. For spring/summer 2007 (c), from the theme of "fighting with an invisible enemy," the motif was a trading card of a fictional fruit monster, and from the theme for autumn/winter 2007 of "connections," the design had a motif of a puzzle.

アパレル / コレクションの招待状　Apparel / Collection Invitation Card
CL：メルシーボークー、mercibeaucoup,　AD：宇津木えり Eri Utsugi　D：庄子結香（カレラ）Yuko Shoji (Karera)
I：阿部伸二（カレラ）Shinji Abe (Karera)　SB：カレラ Karera

c

d

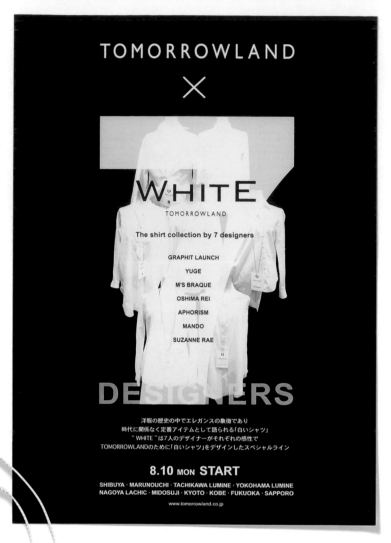

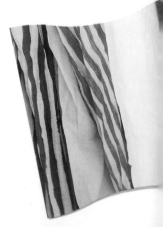

路面店を中心に展開したシャツコレクションの告知

7人のデザイナーとのコラボレーションによるシャツコレクション『WHITE』。『7』の数字をモチーフにデザインした。白シャツの『白』を強調するため『黒』を使用し、Black & Whiteの2トーンカラーでシックなイメージに。フライヤーの『7』の部分をUV印刷にすることで立体感を出し『7』を強調した。

A flyer giving notice of a shirt collection developed for street-level stores

The WHITE shirt collection produced by a collaboration of seven designers. The design contains a motif of the number 7. Black was used to emphasize the white of the white shirts creating a chic look with black and white two–tone colors. The "7" in the flyer was UV-printed for a three-dimensional effect and for additional emphasis of the 7.

アパレル / フェアの告知
Apparel / Event Announcement
CL, AD, D, SB：トゥモローランド TOMORROWLAND Co., Ltd.

斬新なデザインで顧客の開拓を狙ったフェアの告知

アンティークウォッチ＆ジュエリーフェアの告知フライヤー。従来のクラシックなアンティーク時計のイメージを覆す斬新なデザインにすることで、渋谷店ならではの感度の高い人たちの集客を図った。店頭で配布するフライヤーであるため、目を引く形状を意識。ジュエリーの部分に艶ニスを敷くことで高級感を演出した。

A flyer with an innovative design aimed at developing new customers

A flyer giving notice of an antique watch & jewelry fair. The innovative design that overturns the conventional image of a classic antique watch was aimed at the kind of discerning customers that frequent the Shibuya store. As the flyer was produced for distribution in store, the shapes were specifically designed to catch the eye. A sense of quality was produced by applying glossy varnish to the jewellery sections of the flyer.

アパレル / フェアの告知　Apparel / Event Announcement
CL, AD, D, SB：トゥモローランド　TOMORROWLAND Co., Ltd.

接客のツールとしても機能するストールフェアの告知

波形のものは、バリエーション豊富な色や柄が売りのストールを分かりやすく伝えるビジュアルにし、ストールを連想させる波形のカットにより動きを付けた。折り型のものは、ストールの巻き方をイラストタッチで説明。折りたたみ式にし、パタパタ開いたときに数多くの巻き方が見えてくることで、興味をそそる形状にした。

A flyer giving notice of a scarf fair that also functions as a tool for welcoming customers

A scarf with a wave pattern was turned into a visual that conveyed the rich variations of color and pattern in an easy-to-understand way and a die-cut wave pattern associated with the scarf was used to add movement. Examples of the various ways of folding the scarves were explained with illustrations. The flyer was designed to be folded up and to capture the interest of the person unfolding it as the numerous ways of folding the scarves appear from the inside.

アパレル / フェアの告知
Apparel / Event Announcement
CL, AD, D, SB：トゥモローランド　TOMORROWLAND Co., Ltd.

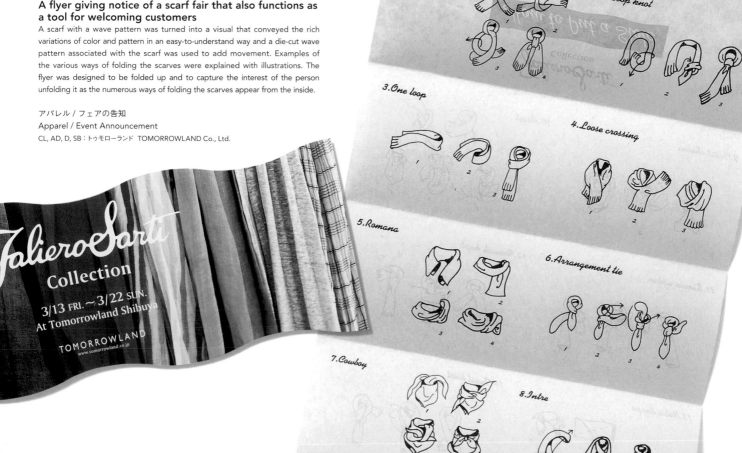

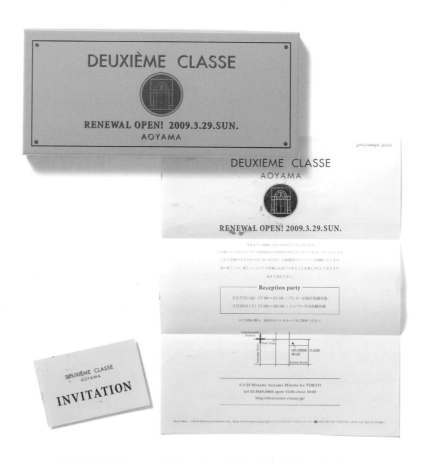

箱を開くとパリの香りが漂うオープニングパーティの招待状

パリのホテルを改装したような店舗に合わせ、パリの香りを封じ込めたインビテーションを
制作。箱の中の花びらには香りを付け、開くと香りが漂う仕掛けに。小さなカードは厚み部
分に天金加工を施し、パーティの案内状は外国のレターセットのような透かし入り用紙にプ
リント。オープンツールはすべて共通イメージを使用した。

An invitation to an opening party with a touch of the fragrance of Paris as the box is opened

The invitation contained a touch of the fragrance of Paris for a store that resembled a
redecorated Parisian hotel. A fragrance that wafted on the air when the box was opened
was applied to the petals inside the box. The thick sections of the small card underwent a
gilding process and the party invitation was printed on watermarked paper that resembled
the stationery used overseas. The same image was used for all the tools produced for the
opening.

アパレル / オープニングパーティの招待状   Apparel / Opening Party Invitation
CL：ドゥーズィエムクラス（ルドーム）DEUXIÈME CLASSE (LEDÔME CO., LTD.)
D：小野寺麻衣 Mai Onodera   DF：ベイクルーズ クリエイティブ BAYCREW'S CO., LTD. CREATIVE DIV.
SB：ベイクルーズ BAYCREW'S CO., LTD.

『JUST TODAY』をテーマに開催した
イベント告知

セレクトショップと多目的スペースを運営する同店の1周年記
念のイベント告知。イベントタイトルは『JUST TODAY・・・
まさに今日』。タイトルロゴにリボンをつけプレゼント感を演出。
柔らかく親しみのあるデザインに仕上げた。

Notice of an event with the theme of Just Today

A notice for an event to celebrate the first anniversary of the
business that operates a boutique and multi-purpose space. The
title of the event is Just Today. The title logo was given the look
of a gift using a ribbon. The result is a design that is soft and
friendly.

セレクトショップ、多目的スペース / イベントの告知
Boutique, Multi-purpose Space / Event Announcement
CL：i-coincidentally　AD, D：宮田裕美詠　Yumiyo Miyata
DF, SB：ストライド　STRIDE

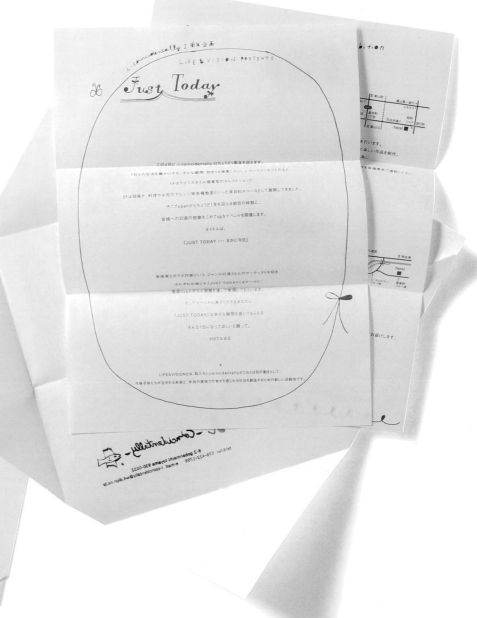

シンプルながら特別感を演出し、
来店を促したセール案内

マニッシュなアイテムに、女らしさを取り入れたユニセックス
なスタイルを提案するセレクトショップのセール案内。シンプ
ルなデザインながら、ミラーの紙に箔押しでコントラストをつ
け、セールの特別感を表現した。

Sale announcement to increase customers to the store, simple yet with a sense of something special

Sale announcement for a select shop offering a unisex style that
incorporates femininity into mannish items. Although the design
is simple, contrast was achieved by foiling the mirror paper to
create the special nature of the sale.

アパレル / セールの案内
Apparel / Sale Announcement
CL：ドゥーズィエムクラス（ルドーム）
DEUXIÈME CLASSE (LEDÔME CO., LTD.)
D：小野寺麻衣　Mai Onodera
DF：ベイクルーズ クリエイティブ　BAYCREW'S CO., LTD. CREATIVE DIV.
SB：ベイクルーズ　BAYCREW'S CO., LTD.

ガーリーなデザインでインパクトを狙った
パーティ招待状

海外誌『LURA』とのコラボレーションパーティ用インビテーション。封筒か
ら雑誌のガーリーな世界観が飛び出すデザインに。型抜き加工を施し、星の
部分は印刷後にシールを貼っている。

**A party invitation aiming for impact with its girly
design**
An invitation to a joint party with the overseas magazine LURA. The girly
worldview of the magazine springs out of the design on the envelope. The
invitation underwent a die-cutting process and a sticker was applied to the
star section after printing.

アパレル / イベントの告知
Apparel / Event Announcement
CL：エディットフォールル（ルドーム）edit. for LuLu (LEDOME CO., LTD.)
D：小野寺麻衣 Mai Onodera
DF：ベイクルーズ クリエイティブ BAYCREW'S CO., LTD. CREATIVE DIV.
SB：ベイクルーズ BAYCREW'S CO., LTD.

うちわとお面でお祭り気分を演出したイベントの招待状

『織姫祭り』というフェアのインビテーションであるため、お祭りのアイテムである "うちわ" をDMに。"お面" と一緒に送り、受け取った人がお祭り気分で楽しくなるような仕掛けにした。両面をフルカラー印刷し、実際に使用できるうちわを制作。

An invitation to an event that creates a festive mood with Japanese fans and masks

As the invitation was to attend a Vega Festival event, the Japanese uchiwa fan used at the event was incorporated into the DM. A mask for the recipient to enjoy the festive mood of the event was sent together with the DM. Both sides of the DM were printed in full color and an uchiwa fan for actual use was also produced.

アパレル / イベントの告知　Apparel / Event Announcement
CL , CD , AD：エディットフォールル（ルドーム）edit. for Lulu (LEDÔME CO., LTD)
D：末廣 歩 Ayumi Suehiro / 石井理恵子 Rieko Ishii　DF, SB：ベイクルーズ BAYCREW'S CO., LTD.

シーズンコレクションのカタログ写真と連動させたオープン告知

シーズンコレクションのカタログ用に撮影した写真を大きめにプリントし、そのままオープン告知DMに。箔押しとリボンでスペシャル感を演出した。

Opening announcement that incorporates photographs from the season's collection catalogues

Slightly larger versions of the photographs shot for the season's collection catalogues were turned into a DM for announcing the opening. A special look was created using foil and ribbons.

アパレル / オープンの告知　Apparel / Opening Announcement
CL：エディットフォールル（ルドーム）edit. for Lulu (LEDÔME CO., LTD.)　D：小野寺麻衣 Mai Onodera
DF：ベイクルーズ クリエイティブ BAYCREW'S CO., LTD. CREATIVE DIV.　SB：ベイクルーズ BAYCREW'S CO., LTD.

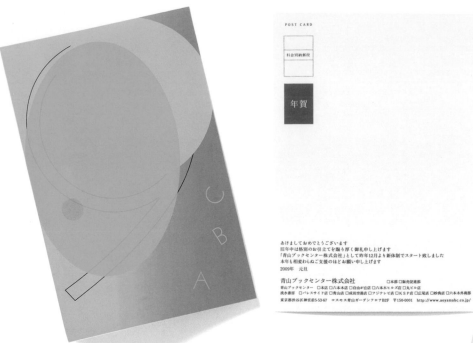

紙面全体で "NEW" を表現した年賀状

新体制で再スタートを切った『青山ブックセンター』の年賀状。メタリック調の特殊紙『スペシャリティーズ』を使用し、"NEW" をストレートに表現した。

A New Year's cards that expresses the word "new" over the entire card

A New Year's card for the Aoyama Book Center that announces a fresh start as a new organization. for its special kind of metallic paper called Specialties was used to express the idea of "new" in a direct way.

書店 / 季節の挨拶状
Bookstore / Seasonal Greetings
CL：青山ブックセンター　AOYAMA BOOK CENTER
AD：山本ヒロキ　Hiroki Yamamoto　DF, SB：マーヴィン　MARVIN

25周年のスペシャル感を演出した コレクションイベントの案内状

レディスラインが25周年を迎えることを記念し、世界中のデザイナーとコラボレーションを行い、展示会を全国で展開。DMはシンボルマークである王冠のロゴを強調するデザインに。トレンドであったドットをモチーフにし、女の子らしさを表現するとともに、イベントが様々な形で展開されていることが伝わるよう意識した。

A fashion collection announcement that incorporates the special feeling of a 25th anniversary

To celebrate the 25th anniversary of the women's line, an exhibition was presented throughout Japan in collaboration with designers from around the world. The design of the DM emphasizes the logo containing a crown, which is the symbol mark. With a motif of dots that were a fashion trend, a feminine quality was expressed and importance attached to conveying the fact that the event was being presented in various forms.

アパレル / コレクションイベントの案内状
Apparel / Fashion Collection Announcement
CL：ビームス BEAMS Co., Ltd.　CD：長柄櫻子 Sakurako Nagara
AD, D：瀧澤仁奈子 Minako Takizawa　DF, SB：ビームス クリエイティブ　BEAMS CREATIVE Inc.

トレンドであるキーワードを紡いで制作した展示会招待状

2009年秋冬コレクションのプレス向け展示会招待状。すべてのレーベルの最新トレンドを、コンセプトを含めて紹介する会であるため、特徴となるキーワードを反映。ジャケットの丈の長さ、キーカラーの赤、ツイード生地などのクラシカルなイメージの中にハイテクを取り入れたアンバランスさなどをミックスして、DMのグラフィックに落とし込んだ。

An invitation to an exhibition incorporating a keywords for trends

An invitation for media personnel to the autumn/winter collection for 2009. As the event was for introducing all the labels and their concepts, keywords for the latest trends were used. Images such as the length of a jacket, the key color of red, asymmetry within a classic design and tweed fabric were incorporated into the graphics for the DM.

アパレル / プレス向けの展示会招待状　Apparel / Fashion Show Invitation for Press
CL：ビームス BEAMS Co., Ltd.　CD：青野賢一 Kenichi Aono
AD, D：瀧澤仁奈子 Minako Takizawa　DF, SB：ビームス クリエイティブ BEAMS CREATIVE Inc.

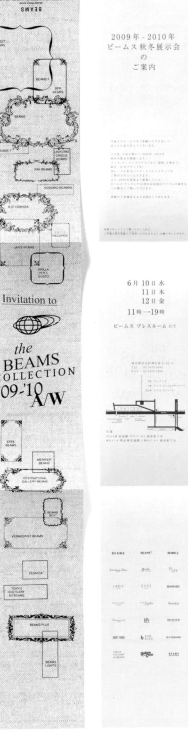

リニューアルしたタワービル全体をモチーフにした内覧会の招待状

『ビームス福岡』グランドオープンの内覧会案内状。背の高い、白い外壁のタワービルそのものをモチーフにしてDMを制作。折りごとに各フロアーのセレクトをイラストで表現し、その世界観を伝えるとともに、フロアマップとしても機能させた。封筒にはざらつきのある紙を使用し、壁の手触りをイメージ。

An invitation to a preview with a motif of an entire renovated tower building

Notice of a preview for the grand opening of Beams Fukuoka. The DM was produced with a motif of a tower with its tall, white outer walls. The boutique shops on each floor were expressed with illustrations between each fold, which as well as conveying the worldview, served also to create a floor map. Coarse paper was used for the envelope to represent the texture of the walls.

アパレル / オープン内覧会の招待状　Apparel / Invitation to a Preview
CL：ビームス BEAMS Co., Ltd.　CD：長友美恵子 Mieko Nagatomo
AD, D：瀧澤仁奈子 Minako Takizawa
I：Miwa Goto　DF, SB：ビームス クリエイティブ BEAMS CREATIVE Inc.

イエローと茄子紺で上質感を演出したリニューアルオープン告知

『原宿BEAMS F』のリニューアルオープン告知DM。店内の壁の色であるイエローとブランドカラーである茄子紺を組み合わせ、きわどい色を使いながら上品に仕上げた。箔押しで老舗感を、封書スタイルで高級感を演出。アイテムのディテールを紹介するカードを同封し、商品ひとつひとつの丁寧なクオリティが伝わるようにした。

Notice of a reopening after renovation that creates a sense of high quality with yellow and dark blue

A DM giving notice of the reopening of Harajuku BEAMS F after renovation. The tricky combination of yellow, the color of the walls, and blue, the brand color, was used but developed in an elegant way. A sense of being a long-established store was created with gold foil and a sense of quality with the DM in the style of a letter. A card containing details about the items was enclosed conveying the careful and individual process of creating the items.

アパレル / オープン告知　Apparel / Opening Announcement
CL：ビームス　BEAMS Co., Ltd.　CD：長友美恵子　Mieko Nagatomo　AD, D：瀧澤仁奈子　Minako Takizawa
I (Cover)：森 眞二 (レバーン)　Shinji Mori (LES BANC Co., Ltd.)　I (Card)：鶴岡恵美 (レバーン)　Megumi Tsuruoka (LES BANC Co., Ltd.)
DF, SB：ビームス クリエイティブ　BEAMS CREATIVE Inc.

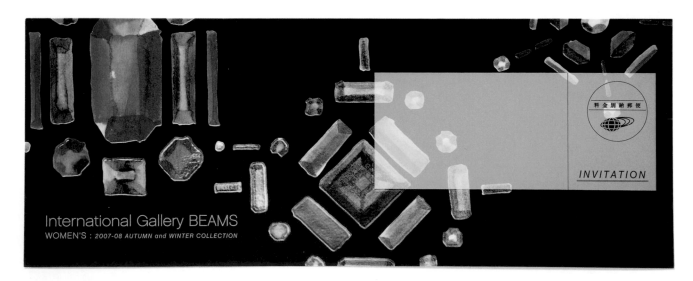

トレンドに合わせたカラーやモチーフでデザインしたDM

2007年秋冬コレクションの案内状。トレンドであったビジュー (石) のイラストで構成。実際にDMを受け取るのは夏であるため、ビジューで冬のキラキラ感を演出するとともに、夏に届いてもスッキリとした印象になるよう工夫した。ビジューに光沢をつけて盛り上げることでリアル感を出し、DM全体に宝石の華やかさを表現。

A DM designed with colors and a motif that align with a fashion trend

Information on the autumn/winter 2007 collection constructed from illustrations of the jewels (stones) that were a fashion trend. Because the DM would be received in summer, it was designed to impart a refreshing impression while using the jewels, to create the sparkling quality of winter. Extra shine was added to the jewels in the DM to create a sense of the real jewels and the gorgeousness of the stones was expressed throughout the DM.

アパレル / 展示会の招待状
Apparel / Fashion Show Invitation
CL：ビームス　BEAMS Co., Ltd.
CD：長柄櫻子　Sakurako Nagara
AD, D, I：瀧澤仁奈子　Minako Takizawa
DF, SB：ビームス クリエイティブ　BEAMS CREATIVE Inc.

ユーザーの心理を付箋で表現した
コレクション告知カタログDM

セレクトショップの秋冬コレクションカタログ。シーズンのはじめに
ファッション雑誌を見ながら何を買おうか思いを巡らせ、気になるもの
に付箋をつけていく、というユーザーの心理をそのまま表現。付箋はす
べて印刷によるオリジナルで印刷工程上の手作業で制作した。

Collection announcement/catalogue DM that uses
tags to expresses the psychology of the user

Catalogue for the Autumn/Winter collection of a boutique store. The
psychology of the user who tags her favorite things as she looks through
the pages of a fashion magazine at the beginning of the season thinking
about what she wants to buy. All the tags are original and produced by a
manual printing process.

洋服販売店 / コレクション告知カタログDM
Clothing Retailer / Collection Announcement
CL：ラタン・イヴ　EVE Group Co., Ltd.　CD：中村富子　Tomiko Nakamura
AD, D：中村 和人　Kazuto Nakamura
D：山田友和　Tomokazu Yamada　DF, SB：ペンギングラフィックス　Penguin Graphics

紙が透け雪の結晶が浮かび上がるホリデーカード

先端をいく企業が集まり、新しいことに積極的な丸の内エリア。挨拶状も王道で
ありながら既視感がなくクオリティーの高いものを目指した。雪の結晶はパチカ
という特殊紙に圧力をかけ制作。シルクのような質感のカードに浮かび上がった
雪の結晶で、上品さの中に意外性を生み出した。

A holiday card made from transparent paper and floating snowflakes

The Marunouchi area where numerous leading-edge companies are based and
the attitude towards new things is positive. For the greeting card, the aim was
to produce something of high quality that had not been seen before. The snow
crystals were created by pressure applied to a special paper called patika. The
floating snowflakes on the card that has a silken texture creates something unique
within the framework of elegance.

不動産 / 季節の挨拶状   Real Estate / Seasonal Greetings

CL：三菱地所 MITSUBISHI ESTATE CO., LTD.   CD：佐藤可士和 Kashiwa Sato
AD, D：細川 剛 Go Hosokawa   D, DF：ツープラトン TWOPLATOON INC.
DF：サムライ SAMURAI INC.   SB：博報堂 HAKUHODO INC.

Ragrise Shibuya Press Party
October 16th(Fri) 18:00-20:00 Shibuya-ku Jinnan 1-12-14
information 03 5456 8890 www.abahouse.co.jp

Ragrise

ブランドイメージをスタイリッシュに演出したパーティ招待状

パリ、ミラノコレクションなどで活躍するデザイナーのスニーカーや高感度なレザーブーツ、東京の今を感じるストリートスニーカーを一堂にセレクトしたショップ『Ragrise渋谷店』。リニューアルオープンのパーティ招待状では、光沢のある紙と『R』の文字を印象的に用い、スタイリッシュでデザイン性の高いブランドイメージをストレートに表現した。

A party invitation that presents the brand image in a stylish way

Select shop Ragrise Shibuya with its range of designer sneakers from Paris and Milan collections, fashion-forward leather boots, and street sneakers that represent contemporary Tokyo. For the invitation to a party to celebrate the reopening of the store after renovation, glossy paper and an impressive letter R were used to express the stylishness and high design of the brand image in a direct way.

アパレル / リニューアルオープンのパーティ招待状
Apparel / Invitation to Reopening Party after Renovation
CL, SB：アバハウスインターナショナル
ABAHOUSE INTERNATIONAL Co., ltd.
AD：米津智之　Tomoyuki Yonezu

若い女性に向けた可愛らしくてインパクトのある展示会案内

若い女性をターゲットとするブランドの展示会案内状であるため、その層に訴求できるような、可愛らしくてインパクトのある質感とレイアウトを心がけた。表面はコンバッソにラメ箔を使用、裏面はグロリアで高級感を演出した。

Information on an exhibition for young women that is cute but powerful

As the information was for an exhibition of a brand whose target group was young women, textures and layout that were cute but also had impact were used in order to market effectively to this group. Lamé foil was used on Combasso on the front and a sense of quality created with Gloria for the back.

アパレル / 展示会の招待状
Apparel / Fashion Show Invitation
CL：三陽商会　SANYO SHOKAI LTD.　D：小池晴子　Haruko Koike
DF, SB：プロップ グラフィック ステーション　PROP GRAPHIC STATION INC.

イルミネーション輝く街をアピールしたプロモーション用DM

クリスマスシーズンに行われたエリアプロモーションの一環として制作。光で描かれたMARUNOUCHI
NIGHTという文字と、街の光をコラージュしたビジュアルでポスターやDM、コースターなど幅広く展開し、『夜も楽しめる街・丸の内』を印象づけた。

Marketing the twinkling street illuminations in a promotional DM

Produced as part of an area promotion conducted during the Christmas season. A poster, DM and coaster
among other things were developed with a collage visual of the words Marunouchi Night written with
light and the light on the streets to create the impression of "Marunochi where the streets are fun at night
too."

不動産 / エリアプロモーションDM   Real Estate / Area Promotion
CL：三菱地所 MITSUBISHI ESTATE CO., LTD.   CD, AD：佐藤可士和 Kashiwa Sato
AD, D：細川 剛 Go Hosokawa   D：林 智徳 Tomonori Hayashi / 山口範久 Norihisa Yamaguchi /
伊藤 剛 Tsuyoshi Ito / 河野吉博 Yoshihiro Kono   CW：坪井 卓 Taku Tsuboi
Producer：菊地孝幸 Takayuki Kikuchi / 横沢英二 Eiji Yokosawa   P：高橋秀行 Hideyuki Takahashi /
岡 祐介 Yusuke Oka   Retouch：波多野 明 Akira Hatano   DF：サムライ SAMURAI INC. /
ツープラトン TWOPLATOON INC.   SB：博報堂 HAKUHODO INC.

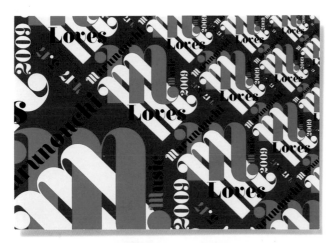
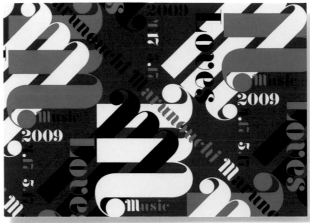

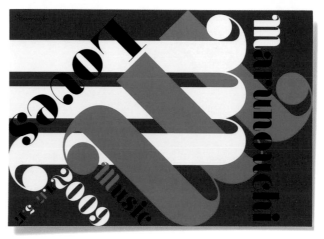

凸凹や質感でシンフォニーを表現した音楽イベントの告知

丸の内で開催された音楽イベントのひとつ『ラ・フォル・ジュルネ 2009』の時期に合わせ、『Marunouchi Loves Music』を意味する『mm』マークでポスターからDMまであらゆるものをジャック。バーコ印刷を用い凸凹や質感の違いをつくり、奥行きある仕上がりにすることでシンフォニーを感じられるようにした。

Expressing the idea of a symphony with bumps and texture for notice of a music event

La Folle Journée Au Japon 2009, one of the music events held in Marunouchi. A range of items from posters to DM were produced using the mm mark that stands for Marunouchi Loves Music. The difference in the bumps and the texture was created using thermographic printing. The idea of the symphony was conveyed by the sophisticated finish.

不動産 / エリアプロモーションDM
Real Estate / Area Promotion
CL：三菱地所 MITSUBISHI ESTATE CO., LTD.
CD, AD：佐藤可士和 Kashiwa Sato
AD, D：細川 剛 Go Hosokawa
D：林 智徳 Tomonori Hayashi / 河野吉博 Yoshihiro Kono
CW：坪井 卓 Taku Tsuboi
DF：サムライ SAMURAI INC. / ツープラトン TWOPLATOON INC.
SB：博報堂 HAKUHODO INC.

DM自体も ART 作品となるようにした
プロモーション告知

ビル内や地下通路にギャラリーがあり、アートイベントも多数開催される丸の内。『COW PARADE Tokyo Marunouchi 2008』や『藝大アーツイン丸の内 2008』の開催に合わせ『ART in Marunouchi』というメッセージを出すことで『アートな街・丸の内』をアピールした。

Promotional notice where the DM itself became an artwork

Marunouchi with galleries inside buildings and in underground thoroughfares and where numerous art events are held. To align with the staging of the COW PARADE Tokyo Marunouchi 2008 and the Geidai Arts in Marunouchi 2008, the idea of "art city Marunouchi" was marketed with the message "ART in Marunouchi."

不動産 / エリアプロモーションDM   Real Estate / Area Promotion
CL：三菱地所 MITSUBISHI ESTATE CO., LTD.
CD, AD：佐藤可士和 Kashiwa Sato
AD, D：細川 剛 Go Hosokawa   D：林 智徳 Tomonori Hayashi
CW：坪井 卓 Taku Tsuboi   DF：サムライ SAMURAI INC. /
ツープラトン TWOPLATOON INC.   SB：博報堂 HAKUHODO INC.

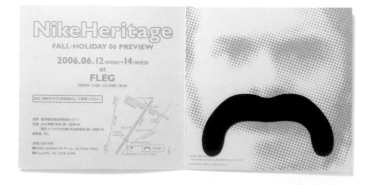

メインウェアをモチーフにした封筒が特徴、展示会の招待状

展示会のメインウェアをモチーフに封筒を制作。招待状には、世界の大きな大会で始めてナイキ
シューズを着用した伝説のアスリート・プリフォンテーン選手にちなんで『口ひげ』を同封。『当日、
同封の"ひげ"を装着の上、ご来場ください』と呼びかけた。

Invitation to an exhibition with the featured wear as the envelope motif

An envelope with a motif of the Nike wear featured in the exhibition was produced. A beard was enclosed in the envelope to make the association with the legendary top athlete Steve Prefontaine who wore the first pair of Nike shoes at a large international sporting event. The invitation calls for guests to wear the beard to the exhibition.

スポーツウェア / 展示会の招待状
Sportswear / Exhibition Invitation

CL：ナイキ・ジャパン　Nike Japan　CD, AD：井上広一　Koichi Inoue
D：佐藤勝昭　Katsuaki Sato　DF, SB：オーイェル　ORYEL

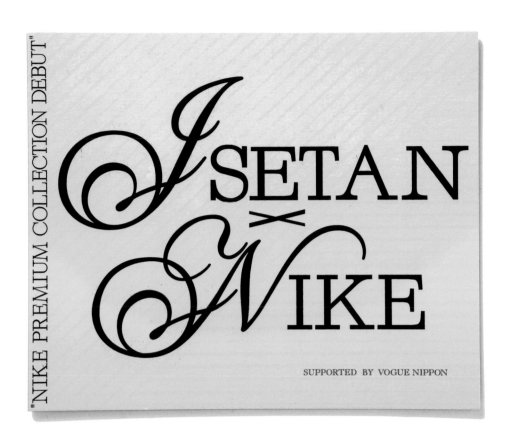

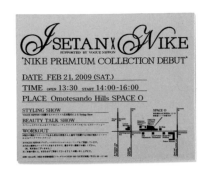

女性らしいロゴが映えるイベントの告知状

VOGUE読者を招待し開催された『ISETAN × NIKE プレミアムコレクション』のDM。ファッションショー、トークショー、エクササイズなど内容豊富なイベントをコレクションの中心カラーである明るいイエローとリフレクター（光る素材）をイメージしたニス加工等で表現。タイトルロゴには女性らしくしなやかな曲線を取り入れた。

A feminine logo to set off notice of an event

A DM for the ISETAN X NIKE Premium Collection to which Vogue readers were invited. A collection theme color of bright yellow and varnish was used to express the content-rich event that includes fashion shows, talk shows and exercise. Feminine, supple curves were incorporated into the title logo.

コンセプトショップ / イベントの告知
Concept Shop / Event Announcement
CL：ナイキ・ジャパン Nike Japan　AD, D, SB：大島慶一郎 Keiichiro Oshima

店頭ツールとしてもDMとしても活用できる新商品の案内

蛇腹タイプの店頭ツールを1枚ずつ切り離して使えるようにし、DMとしても活用。商品ビジュアルをメインに、春夏コレクションらしく清涼感あるデザインで統一。ニスによるタイポグラフィがアクセントとなっている。

New product information that can be used either as a store tool or a DM

The accordion-style in-store promotion can be torn off and used separately or as a DM. With a central visual of the product, unity has been achieved with a refreshing design befitting of a spring and summer collection. The varnished typography provides an accent.

スポーツウェア / 新商品の案内状　Sportswear / New Merchandise Announcement
CL：フェニックス Phenix　AD, D：井上広一 Koichi Inoue　P：西 将隆 Masataka Nishi
DF, SB：オーイェル ORYEL

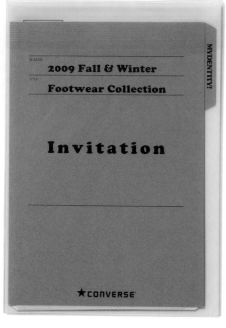

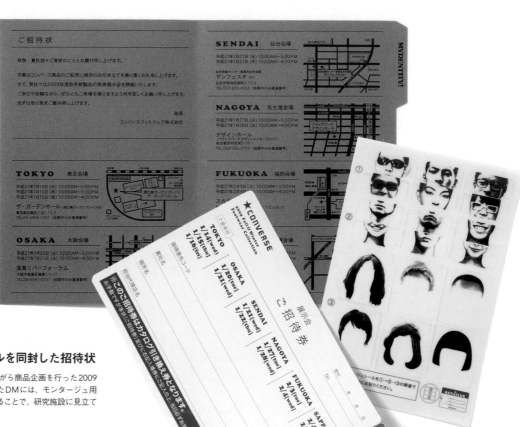

会場演出との連動を狙い、モンタージュ用シールを同封した招待状

ターゲットユーザーである若者のリアルな姿を広く深くリサーチしながら商品企画を行った2009年秋冬のシーズンテーマ『MYDENTITY！』。ファイルをイメージしたDMには、モンタージュ用のシールを同封し、来場者の名札となる部分に自由に貼れるようにすることで、研究施設に見立てた会場の演出と連動したテーマ訴求を行った。

An invitation with montage stickers enclosed aimed at creating a link with the production design of the venue

The MYDENTITY! season theme for autumn/winter 2009 product design that conducts research on the real world of young people who are the target users. Montage stickers where enclosed with the DM produced in the image of a file and by being to apply the stickers to the section for the visitor's business card, the idea of linking of the theme with the production design of the venue was realized

シューズの企画、開発、販売 / 展示会の招待状
Design, Development and Sale of Footwear / Fashion Show Invitation
CL, SB：コンバースフットウェア　CONVERSE FOOTWEAR CO., LTD.　DF：エム・ツウ・カンパニー　M2 COMPANY

蝶ネクタイをデザインし、展示会の演出と連動させた招待状

ドレスアップとドレスダウンという相反する要素をミックスしながら商品企画を行った2010年春夏のシーズンテーマ『Dress Code 1/2』。モノトーンのだまし絵で会場を構成し、シューズを展示。来場者に招待状を首から提げてもらい、全員が蝶ネクタイを付けているかのように見せることで会場演出と連動。

An invitation where a bow tie was connected to the production design of the exhibition

Mixing the contradictory elements of dress-up and dress-down, the Dress Code ½ season theme for spring/summer 2010 product design. The shoes were displayed in a venue constructed with monotone trompe l'oeil. Visitors to the event were asked to hang the invitation around their necks making it appear as if everyone was wearing a bow tie, which linked to the production design of the venue.

シューズの企画、開発、販売 / 展示会の招待状
Design, Development and Sale of Footwear / Fashion Show Invitation
CL, SB：コンバースフットウェア　CONVERSE FOOTWEAR CO., LTD.
DF：デキスギ　DEKISUGI CORPORATION

走るサロンに、走れ！
INVITATION TO SALON BUS

CANVAS CHEVRON STAR HI
price: ¥6,800 color: ■■

PRO LEATHER 76 HI
price: ¥9,800 color: ■■

箱の内側に招待文を記載したBOXタイプの案内状

ロンドンバスをカスタムした『移動式サロン』で実施されたプロモーション用に制作したDM。バス内で商品の展示とスタイリングの提案を行った。商品をきちんと見てもらいたいという思いと、もらった人がわくわくできる案内状を目指し、中にはチケット型のカタログを入れ、箱の内側に直接招待文を記載した。

A box-type notice written in the form of an invitation on the inside of a box

A DM produced for promotional activity conducted in a "moving salon" using a customized London bus. Suggestions were made for the display and styling of the products inside the bus. The aim of the notice was to make sure that people looked at the products properly and that people were excited to receive the information notice.

シューズの企画、開発、販売 / キャンペーンのプレス向け案内状
Design, Development and Sale of Footware / Campaign Notice for Media
CL：コンバースフットウェア CONVERSE FOOTWEAR CO., LTD.
CD, Planner：勢井浩二郎 Kojiro Sei AD：本村耕平 Kohei Motomura
D：村井保介 Yasusuke Murai DF, SB：デキスギ DEKISUGI CORPORATION

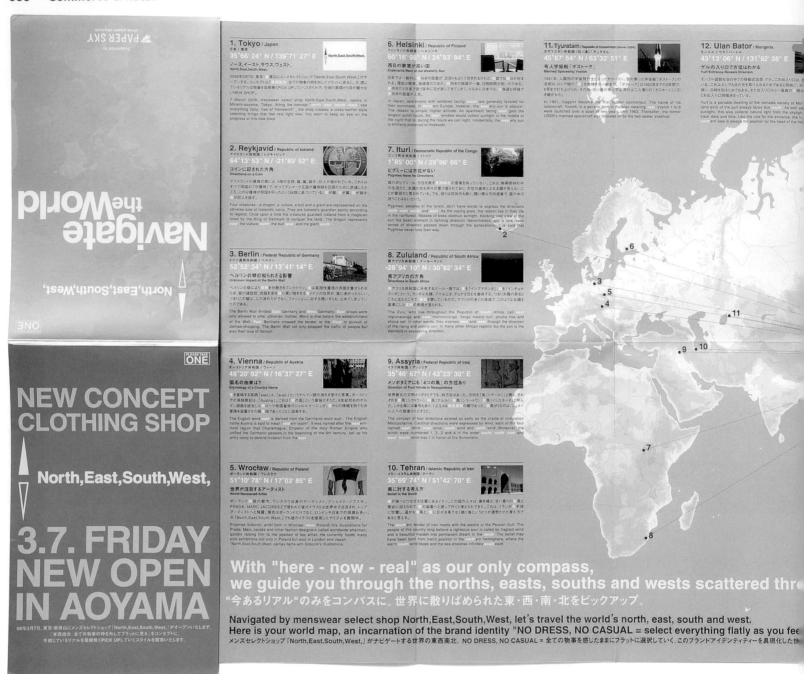

a

ブランドやショップへのより強い印象付けを意識したDM

(a) はブランドカラーであるモノトーンを軸とし、地図のような形状にデザイン。コンセプトの『東西南北、全ての物事の枠を外してフラットに見る』をもとに、旅行誌『PAPER SKY』による『東西南北』にまつわるコンテンツで構成した。(b) は圧着ハガキの中面にメイン写真を配置し、『めくる』工程による印象付けを狙った。

A DM that wanted a strong impression for the brand and the shop

For (a), the design centered on a monotone, the brand color, and was in a form that resembled a map. Based on the concept of "To the north, south, east and west, remove the frame from all things to see the world in one dimension," the DM was constructed with contents that included the "north, south, east and west" of the travel magazine Paper Sky. For (b), main photographs were arranged in the center of an adhesive postcard with the aim of creating an impression by the peeling back of the adhesive layer.

アパレル / 新コンセプトブランドの案内、ショップオープンの告知
Apparel / Announcement for a New Concept Brand & Shop Opening
CL：ルドーム　LEDÔME CO., LTD.　D：原野 拓　Taku Harano
P (b)：久保田育央 (オウル カンパニー)　Ikuo Kubota (OWL COMPANY)
DF：ベイクルーズ クリエイティブ　BAYCREW'S CO., LTD. CREATIVE DIV.
Editing (a)：ニーハイメディア・ジャパン　Knee High Media Japan Inc.
SB：ベイクルーズ　BAYCREW'S CO., LTD.

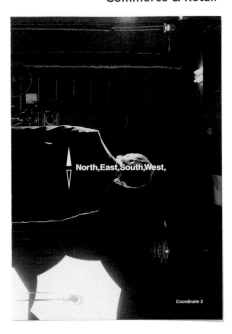

b

緑や野鳥の多い新店舗の街をイメージしたDM

『JOURNAL STANDARD ルミネ立川店』のオープン告知。オープン地である東京・立川（緑、野鳥の多い街）をイメージしデザインした。

A DM with an image of the new store's street full of greenery and wild birds

Notice of the opening of the JOURNAL STANDARD LUMINE Tachikawa store. The design incorporated an image of Tachikawa, Tokyo where the opening was held (a street full of greenery and wild birds).

アパレル / 新店オープン告知
Apparel / New Store Opening Announcement
CL：ジャーナルスタンダード（JS.ワークス）
JOURNAL STANDARD (JS.WORKS CO., LTD.)
D：原野 拓　Taku Harano
DF：ベイクルーズ クリエイティブ　BAYCREW'S CO., LTD. CREATIVE DIV.
SB：ベイクルーズ　BAYCREW'S CO., LTD.

新店舗への期待感を表現した
オープニングパーティの招待状

『JOURNAL STANDARD札幌店』のリニューアルパーティ招待状。新しくなった店舗のパーティということで、のぞき窓からロゴ入りのコルクボードを覗かせて、ワクワク感と期待感を表現。7インチレコードスリーブを封筒として使用した。

An invitation to an opening party that expresses the sense of anticipation for the new store

An invitation to the reopening of the JOURNAL STANDARD Sapporo store after renovation. As the party was for the newly renovated store, a glimpse was given through a peephole of a corkboard containing the logo to express a sense of excitement and anticipation. A 7" record sleeve was used as an envelope.

アパレル / オープニングパーティの招待状
Apparel / Opening Party Invitation
CL：ジャーナルスタンダード（JS.ワークス）
JOURNAL STANDARD (JS.WORKS CO., LTD.)
AD, D：山川伊久　Iku Yamakawa
DF：ベイクルーズ クリエイティブ　BAYCREW'S CO., LTD. CREATIVE DIV.
SB：ベイクルーズ　BAYCREW'S CO., LTD.

テーマであるリバティープリントをアピールしたイベント告知
リバティープリントのイベント告知用フライヤー。大判サイズで生地のプリントを再現し、筒状に丸めて白いゴムで止め配布した。

An event announcement that makes an appeal using a Liberty print that is the theme
A leaflet giving notice of a Liberty print event. A large-size reproduction of a fabric print was made, rolled into a tube shape, fastened with white elastic and distributed.

アパレル / イベントの告知
Apparel / Event Announcement
CL, CD：スピックアンドスパン（フレームワークス）
Spick and Span (FRAMEWORKS)　D：栃原 愛　Ai Tochihara
DF：ベイクルーズ クリエイティブ
BAYCREW'S CO., LTD. CREATIVE DIV.
SB：ベイクルーズ　BAYCREW'S CO., LTD.

店内装飾の一部をビジュアル化した
インビテーション

『ランド オブ トゥモロー 丸の内店』のオープンDM。実際に店内装飾として使用されている階段の手すりの素材感を平面で表現。設計の際に使われたアーティスト "リサ" の絵をイラスト化し、来店者に向け、より強い印象づけを図った。イラスト部分にUV加工を施すことにより、実際の手すりのような立体感を出している。

An invitation turning a part of the shop decor into a visual
A DM for the opening of the Land of Tomorrow Marunouchi store. A sense of the materials used for the staircase banister that was part of the store's décor was expressed as a flat surface. The painting of the artist Lisa used during the design process was turned into an illustration with the aim of producing a greater impact on visitors to the store. The illustration underwent a UV process to produce the three-dimensional effect of the actual banister.

アパレル / オープンの告知
Apparel / Opening Announcement
CL, AD, D, SB：トゥモローランド TOMORROWLAND Co., Ltd.

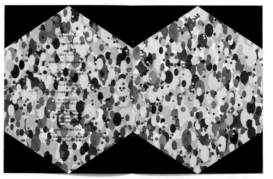

カラフルな世界でコレクションテーマを
表現した招待状

モデルとしても活躍するSachiがデザインを手がけるシューズブラン
ド。コレクション毎にテーマを設け、会場からDMまで独自の世界観を
演出している。『お菓子のなる魔法の木 in the Black Gift Box』をテー
マとした展示会では、黒い箱の中に広がるカラフルな世界をコンセプト
にDMを制作した。

An invitation that expresses the theme of the collection with a colorful world

A shoe brand designed by Sachi who also works as a model. A theme
was established for each collection and a unique worldview created for
everything from the venue to the DM. For the exhibition that featured the
theme "in the Black Gift Box," a DM was produced based on the concept
of a colorful world contained in a black box.

アパレル、レディースシューズブランド / 展示会の招待状
Apparel, Lady's Shoes Brand / Fashion Show Invitation
CL：アトミックグリーン Atomic Green　Art Work, SB：西舘朋央 Tomoo Nishidate
AD：山田信男（CENTRAL PARK）Nobuo Yamada（CENTRAL PARK）

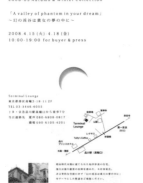 

AtomicGreen
2008-09 Autumn & Winter Collection

『A valley of phantom in your dream』
～幻の渓谷は貴女の夢の中に～

2008.4.15(火) 4.18(金)
10:00-19:00 for buyer & press

『幻の渓谷』をテーマに制作したレディースシューズのコレクションDM

『幻の渓谷はあなたの夢の中に』をテーマに開催されたコレクションの招待状。展示会場の実際の扉を絵にしたコラージュを用い、会場との連動性をもたせた。箱の中は全体に苔をひき、シューズデザイナーSachiの横顔の影、地図を切り抜いた鳥、水をイメージしたビー玉で同展示会の世界を演出した。

A DM for a ladies shoes collection based on the theme of "the imaginary valley is in your dreams"

An invitation to a collection show taking "the imaginary valley is in your dreams" as its theme. A collage of pictures of the actual door to the exhibition was used to link the DM to the venue. The inside of the box was lined with moss, with the shadow of the shoe-designer Sachi's profile, birds cut out of a map, and marbles representing water added to dramatize the world of the exhibition.

アパレル、レディースシューズブランド / 展示会の招待状
Apparel, Lady's Shoes Brand / Fashion Show Invitation
CL：アトミックグリーン Atomic Green   Art Work, SB：西舘朋央 Tomoo Nishidate

DM毎に異なる切手とティーバッグを同封した展示会の招待状

コレクションテーマは『CITY WOMAN VIEW 都会に住む女の見た風景』。招待状はそれぞれに異なる外国の切手とお菓子の包み紙、紅茶のティーバッグを同封。透明の封筒を使用し、中身を見せることで興味を惹くDMとなった。

Invitation to an exhibition containing a different stamp and tea bag for each DM

The theme of the collection was "City Woman View." A different foreign stamp, sweet wrapper and tea bag were enclosed with each of the invitations. Transparent envelopes were used to attract interest in their contents.

アパレル、レディースシューズブランド / 展示会の招待状
Apparel, Lady's Shoes Brand / Fashion Show Invitation
CL：アトミックグリーン Atomic Green
Art Work, SB：西舘朋央 Tomoo Nishidate

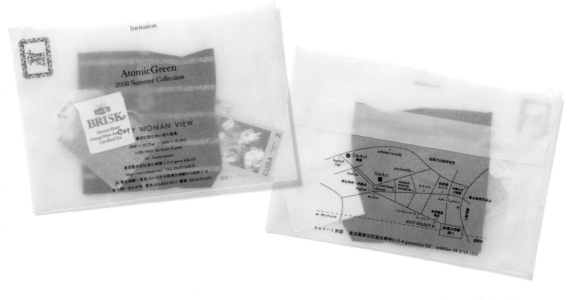

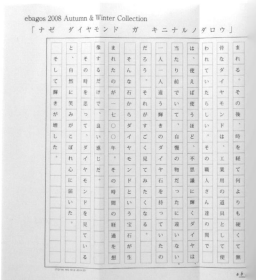

ebagos 2008 Autumn & Winter Collection

ドライフラワーを同封したオープニングパーティの招待状

新しいコスメブランド『THREE』の告知＆招待状。『モダンで自由な女性像』と『効果的な天然原料の提案』というブランドコンセプトをCIカラーのグレーを寸法違いの折りで立体的に表現。さらにドライフラワーを同封することで、インパクトと安心感の両立を目指した。

Invitation to opening party with dried flowers enclosed

Notice of the new cosmetics brand, Three, and an invitation. The concept of a "modern, free woman" and "offering effective natural ingredients" is expressed in a three-dimensional way using folds in different sizes in the CI color of grey. Additional impact and a sense of comfort was the aim of enclosing the dried flowers.

化粧品 / オープニングパーティの招待状　Cosmetics / Opening Party Invitation
CL：アクロ ACRO　AD, D, SB：浜田武士 Takeshi Hamada

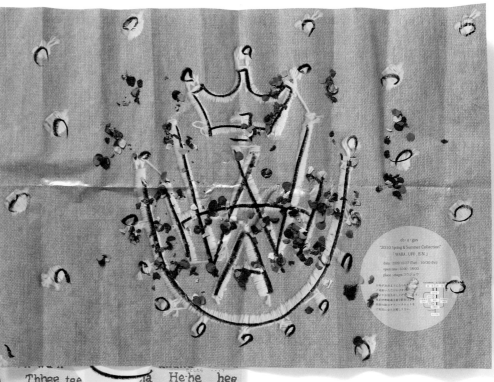

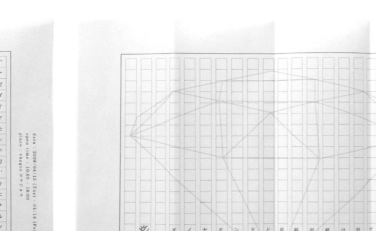

楽しい仕掛けでテーマを表現した展示会の招待状

2010年春夏コレクションの展示会招待状。『WHA UFU E-N』という様々な感情の動きをテーマとし、表面にはそれらの英字で構成したロゴを、裏面には感情表現の言葉を央字で並べ、日本語の詩を配した。開くと、ビックリ箱のように色紙が出てくる仕掛け。左端には一輪のバラも置き、手にとってうれしいDMに仕上げた。

Invitation to a fashion show that expresses the theme with a fun device

Invitation to a fashion show for the 2010 spring/summer collection. Featuring the theme of Japanese sounds for various emotions, the logo that incorporates those sounds written with English-language characters was placed on the front and on the back, the words to express emotions using English-language characters as well as a Japanese poem. When the invitation is opened, colored paper springs out much like a Jack-in-the-box. A rose was placed at the left-hand side to delight the recipient.

アパレル / 展示会の招待状　Apparel / Fashion Show Invitation
CL, SB：エバゴス　eb・a・gos　AD, D：曽我部美加　Mika Sogabe

原稿用紙をモチーフにした
展示会の招待状

手作業で作られる個性的なバッグを中心としたブランド『eb・a・gos』の2009年秋冬コレクションの展示会招待状。『ナゼ ダイヤモンド ガ キニナルノダロウ』というテーマから、原稿用紙を導き出した。

An invitation to a fashion show with a motif of manuscript paper

An invitation to a fashion show for the 2009 autumn/winter eb・a・gos brand that specializes in unique handmade bags. Manuscript paper was used to lead to the theme "What is it about diamonds that attracts you so?"

アパレル / 展示会の招待状
Apparel / Fashion Show Invitation
CL, SB：エバゴス　eb・a・gos
AD, D：曽我部美加　Mika Sogabe

アンティークドイリーレースを
モチーフにした『日傘展』の招待状

600mm×480mmサイズの紙を畳み、宛名シールで封を
する形状。裏面は、展示会の日傘のコンセプトである一点
物のアンティークドイリーレースを散らしたように、淡い
青緑色で印刷。畳むと幾十にも重なり、広げてみたくなる
ようなデザインに。表面には、全国数カ所で開催するイメー
ジが伝わるように日本地図を印刷。

An invitation to an umbrella exhibition
with a motif of antique doily lace

A sheet of 600mm x 480mm paper was folded and sealed
with an address seal. The back of the invitation was printed
with a light bluish green to make the one-or-a-kind antique
doily lace, the concept of sun umbrellas exhibited, appear
scattered. The design encouraged the unfolding of the
invitation that had been folded into multiple layers. A
map of Japan was printed on the front to convey the idea
that the exhibition was being held in several locations
throughout Japan.

傘屋 / 展示会の招待状
Umbrella Brand / Exhibition Invitation
CL：イイダ傘店 Iida Umbrella　SB：驚 EI Co.Ltd.

花柄の世界観を印象づける『雨傘展』の招待状

『イイダ傘店』が2009年秋に催した『雨傘展』の招待状。展示会のメインデザインである
花柄の世界観が、DMを受け取った人にさりげなく伝わるよう、封筒の内側にカラーで模様
を印刷。会場毎のカードはシンプルに日時場所だけを単色で印刷し、ポイントとしてカード
の側面一辺に、花柄に使われている色の絵の具を塗った。

An invitation to an umbrella exhibition that makes an impression
with a floral-pattern worldview

An invitation to an umbrella exhibition held by Iida Umbrella in autumn 2009. A pattern was
printed in color on the inside of the envelope so as to convey a floral-pattern worldview, the
central design of the exhibition, to recipients of the DM in a casual, relaxed way. The cards for
each exhibition venue were simple with only the time and place printed in a single color. Paint
in the same colors used for the floral pattern was applied along one edge of the card.

傘屋 / 展示会の招待状　Umbrella Brand / Exhibition Invitation
CL：イイダ傘店 Iida Umbrella　SB：驚 EI Co.Ltd.

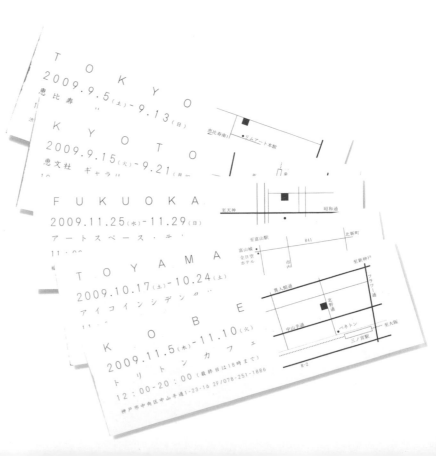

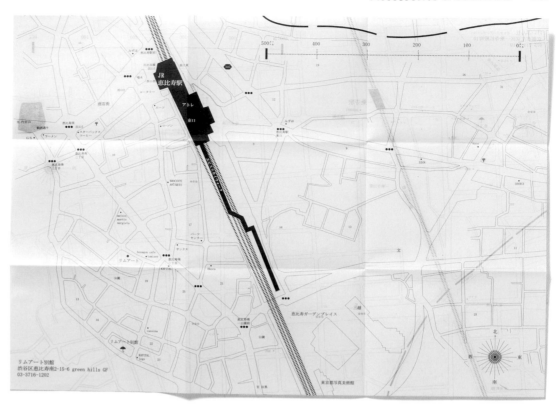

会場の近所も散歩できるよう、地図に仕立てた『雨傘展』の招待状

傘の展示会だとすぐにわかるように、封筒全面に傘のイラストを印刷。展示会には、休日に散歩がてら来場する一般の人も多いため、中身は大きめの地図に仕立て、手に持って近所を歩いてもらえるよう制作した。

An invitation to an umbrella exhibition that resembles a map of the neighborhood around the exhibition venue

An illustration of umbrellas was printed over the entire surface of the envelope so that the exhibition was immediately recognizable as an umbrella exhibition. As many members of the public arrive at the exhibition on foot on their day off, the inside of the invitation resembles a rather large map so that patrons can stroll around the neighborhood map in hand.

傘屋 / 展示会の招待状
Umbrella Brand / Exhibition Invitation
CL：イイダ傘店 Iida Umbrella
SB：騎 EI Co.Ltd.

傘の生地と同じ印刷を施し、世界観を伝える『日傘展』の招待状

生地からオリジナルで制作して傘づくりを行っている丁寧な仕事をDMにも反映。花柄の『送り』（パターンデザインで次につながっていくこと）の部分をデザインに取り込み、印刷。生地のシルクスクリーンと同様、DMにも一色ごとに印刷色を載せるスクリーン印刷を施し、その世界観を表現した。

An invitation to an umbrella exhibition printed with the same pattern as an umbrella and conveying a worldview

The DM also reflected the painstaking work involved with the dyeing of the fabric to produce an original umbrella. Sections of a floral pattern were incorporated into the design and then printed. The DM was screen-printed in the same way as the silk-screen printing of the umbrella fabric with the inks applied one at a time for each color in the pattern to express the store's worldview.

傘屋 / 展示会の招待状
Umbrella Brand / Exhibition Invitation
CL：イイダ傘店 Iida Umbrella
SB：騎 EI Co.Ltd.

NYのニュースペーパーをモチーフにしたオープン告知

ニューヨークのイーストヴィレッジでアボセカリー（調剤薬局）として誕生したキールズ。1851年の創業以来、天然由来成分を配合したクオリティの高い製品を提供するキールズを、NYの新聞をモチーフに表現。社会貢献を重要視する同社らしく、リサイクルペーパーを使用し制作された。

Store-opening announcement with a New York newspaper motif

Kiehl's, an apothecary founded in New York's East Village in 1851 that provides high-quality products containing ingredients sourced from nature. A New York newspaper was used as a motif. Recycled paper was used to represent the value placed by the business on "giving to the community."

化粧品 / オープン告知
Cosmetics / Opening Announcement
CL, DF, SB：キールズ Kiehl's Since 1851

ポップなイメージを表現した
オープニングパーティの招待状

クロックスがもつポップでカラフルなイメージを意識し制作した
オープニングパーティの招待状。シューズの画像を印刷し型抜きし
たチケットは、質感や履き心地のよさも伝わる仕上がりとなった。

**A pop look for an invitation to an opening
party**
An invitation to an opening party that incorporates the colorful, pop
image for which crocs is known. The ticket onto which the image of
a pair of shoes was printed and then cut out conveys the texture and
the comfort of a pair of crocs.

靴メーカー / オープニングパーティの招待状
Shoemaker / Opening Party Invitation
CL：クロックス crocs   AD, D：山崎弘幸 Hiroyuki Yamazaki
DF, SB：ノーザングラフィックス Northern Graphics

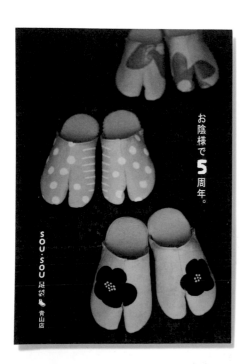

シンプルなデザインでブランドイメージを伝えた
5周年の挨拶＆新商品の案内状

日本の伝統の軸線上にあるモダンデザインをコンセプトにオリジナル
テキスタイルを作成・販売する京都のブランド『SOU・SOU』。5周
年の挨拶とともに、新商品の手描きスリッパを紹介。商品のイメージ
がダイレクトに伝わるよう、写真を活かし、シンプルに仕上げた。

**Greetings on the fifth anniversary and
information on new products that conveys the
brand image via a simple design**
The SOU SOU brand from Kyoto that produces and sells original
textiles, based on the concept of modern design on the axis of
Japanese tradition. Hand-drawn versions of pairs of slippers, new
products were presented together with greetings on the fifth
anniversary. Photographs and a simple design were used to convey the
product image in a straightforward way.

製造・小売業 / 5周年の挨拶状、新商品の案内状
Manufacturer , Retail /
Fifth-anniversary Greetings, Information on New Products
CL, CD, SB：SOU・SOU

顧客のタイプ別にサンプル贈呈した
新ファンデーションの案内状

5年ぶりの商品リニューアルにともない『エクスボーテからお贈りするプレゼント』をテーマに制作。顧客データをもとに8パターンのサンプルキットを用意し、バリアブルプリントでお客様に合わせてレター内容も変更した。外箱にかけられたブランドカラーのリボンは『プレゼント』の気持ちをこめ手作業で行われた。

Notice of a new foundation where customers are presented with a sample gift according to customer type

Based on the theme "a gift from Ex:beaute" to coincide with the first product upgrade in five years. Eight kinds of sample kits were prepared on the basis of customer data, matched to customer types using variable prints and letter content. The ribbon in the brand color was applied by hand to the outer box to enhance the sense of a "present."

化粧品 / 新商品の案内状   Cosmetics / New Merchandise Announcement
CL, SB：マードゥレクス MARDREX

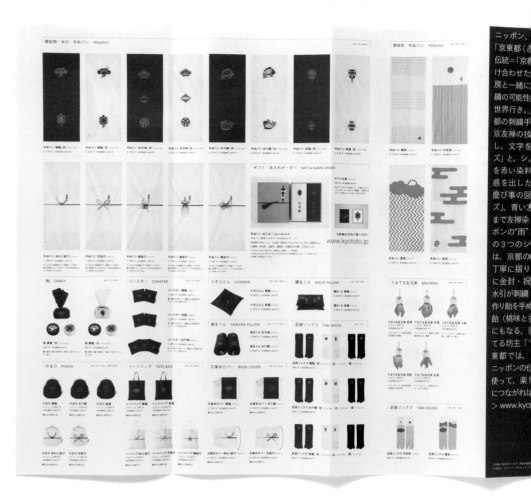

ニッポン、京都発、東京経由〜世界行き。「京東都（きょうとうと）」は、ニッポンの伝統＝「京都」とニッポンの今＝「東京」を掛け合わせたブランドネーム。京都の刺繍工房と一緒に、新しい文化継承のかたち・刺繍の可能性を考える「京都発、東京経由〜世界行き。」の、刺繍ブランドです。京東都の刺繍手ぬぐいは、日本の四季の柄を京友禅の技法『かちん染め（墨）』で表現し、文字を刺繍した「かちん染めシリーズ」と、シルクを精錬する時に出る繭の粉

東都では、ニッポンの形や音の美しさを、ニッポンの伝統技術を、見て、聞いて、感じ、使って、楽しむことで、新しい文化の継承につながればと思っています。
> www.kyototo.jp

のしをつけ贈答品に見立てた『京東都』の商品案内

京都の刺繍工房と一緒に新しい文化継承のかたち・刺繍の可能性を追求する刺繍ブランド『京東都』。『京都発、東京経由〜世界行き』をメインテーマに様々な商品を展開。シリーズごとに見やすくまとめながら、手ぬぐいの良さや刺繍の繊細さを伝えられるようにした。

Kyototo product information featuring a gift with noshi decoration

Embroidery brand Kyototo works with a studio in Kyoto to discover new forms of cultural inheritance and the potential of embroidery. Kyototo has developed various products based on its main theme "Departing Kyoto for the world, via Tokyo." The organization of each product series is simple so it is easy to find what you are looking for but the quality of the hand towels and the delicate embroidery have also been conveyed.

衣料品 / 商品の案内
Clothing / Product Information
CL：ドゥオモ DUOMO CO., LTD.
CD, AD, D, P, I, DF, SB：スリーミン
3MIN. COMPANY. LIMITED

女性らしいやわらかなデザインで展開した
展示会の招待状

展示会のテーマは『hug 〜やわらかく、あたたかく、つつみこむ〜』。商品の提案するhugのカタチだけでなく、環境へのやさしさ、あたたかさなど、地球へのhugというメッセージもこめられている。すっきりと女性らしいデザインながら、展示会のテーマが伝わるような招待状を心がけた。

A mild, feminine design for an invitation to an exhibition

The theme of the exhibition was "hug ... wrapping you up softly and warmly." The invitation incorporates the same "hug" idea as the product but also the environmentally friendly and warm idea of "hugging the earth." The aim was a design that was fresh and feminine but also conveyed the theme of the exhibition.

パンティストッキング、ソックス、インナーウェア / 展示会の招待状
Pantyhose, Socks, Undergarments / Fashion Show Invitation
CL, SB：アツギ ATSUGI CO., LTD.
AD：東 俊一郎 (ギャルド ユウ・エス・ピイ) Shunichiro Higashi (GARDE U・S・P Co., Ltd.) /
徳井麻里子 (ギャルド ユウ・エス・ピイ) Mariko Tokui (GARDE U・S・P Co., Ltd.)
D：一尾りか Ricca Ichio Printing：CHOCOLATE CO., LTD.

時計のリストバンドをモチーフにした展示会の招待状

1984年アメリカに誕生したカジュアルウォッチ『フォッシル』の展示会招待状。コンセプトである古き良き時代の"アメリカン・ヴィンテージ"をベースに、時計のリストバンドをイメージし、立体感のあるDMに仕上げた。

An invitation to an exhibition with watchband motif

An invitation to an exhibition of the Fossil casual watches brand founded in the United States in 1984. Based on the concept of the "American vintage " of the good old days, an image of a watchband was used to create a three-dimensional effect.

時計ブランド / 展示会の招待状
Watch Maker / Exhibition Invitation
CL：フォッシルジャパン FOSSIL JAPAN Inc. D：吉田望絵 Moe Yoshida
DF, SB：プロップ グラフィック ステーション PROP GRAPHIC STATION INC. Agency：コスモ・コミュニケーションズ Cosmo Communications Inc.

ムーブメントのデザインをモチーフにして、伝統の機能美を現代的に表現したイベント告知

卓越した技術を誇る高級時計ブランド『オーデマ・ピゲ』のイベント案内。デザインには、職人の魂が宿っている時計の設計図を使用し、『外観だけでなく、内部のパーツも美しい』というメッセージを込めた。箔押しやグロス PP などを施し、2 次加工で高級感を演出した。

Notice for an event that expresses the beauty of classic function using design of movement as a motif
Information on an event for the Audemars Piguet high-quality watch brand. The design used the technical drawings for a watch that captures the soul of the craftsman to convey the message that "the outside is beautiful but so is the inside." Foiling and gloss film lamination was chosen and a sense of quality added through secondary processing.

時計ブランド / イベントの告知　Watch Maker / Event Announcement
CL：オーデマ ピゲ ジャパン　AUDEMARS PIGUET JAPAN　D：丸井元子　Motoko Marui　DF, SB：プロップ グラフィック ステーション　PROP GRAPHIC STATION INC.

流れ星でモダンな感性を演出したオープニングパーティの招待状

老舗ジュエラー『モーブッサン』銀座店のオープニングパーティ案内。歴史を伝えるためブック形式を採用。『銀座に流れ星』というコンセプトのもと、星に見立てたロゴマークのアウトラインを型抜きし、モダンさを表現。封筒には光沢のある紙を使って星の印象を強調し、DM開封時に星が降り注ぐようロゴを配置した。

An invitation to an opening party that creates a modern sensibility with shooting stars

An invitation to a party for the opening of the Ginza branch of the long-established jeweller, Mauboussin. A book format was used to convey a sense of history. Based on the concept of "shooting stars in the Ginza," the logo was designed to resemble a star and then cut out around its outline to create a modern look. Glossy paper was used for the envelope to make the star even more impressive and the logo placed so that the stars appeared to falling when the DM was opened.

ジュエリー / オープニングパーティの招待状　Jewerly / Opening Party Invitation
CL：モーブッサン ジャパン MAUBOUSSIN JAPAN　CD：美澤 修 Osamu Misawa　AD, D：竹内 衛 Mamoru Takeuchi　DF, SB：omdr omdr Co., Ltd.

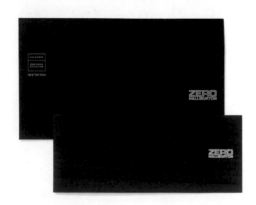

会場イメージと連動させたデザインで仕上げたパーティの案内状

1938年の設立以来、数々の実績と逸話を持つZERO HALLIBURTONのケース。直線的なデコレーションや証明で新世ZERO HALLIBURTONの世界観を演出した会場イメージと連動させたDMを制作。黒を基調にスタイリッシュなデザインで仕上げた。

Notice of a party designed to link to an image of the party venue

A case by Zero Halliburton, which since its establishment in 1938 has accumulated many successes and anecdotes. The DM is designed to link to an image of the linear decoration and lighting at the party venue where the new-generation Zero Halliburton worldview will be presented, and finished with a stylish design in the basic tone of black.

旅行バッグ、小物などの製造・卸 / プレスローンチパーティの案内状
Luggage, Accessories Maker and Wholesale / Notice of Press Launch Party

CL：エース ACE Co., Ltd.　CD, Planner：勢井浩二郎（デキスギ）Kojiro Sei (DEKISUGI)　D：風間重美 Emi Kazama
SB：デキスギ DEKISUGI CORPORATION

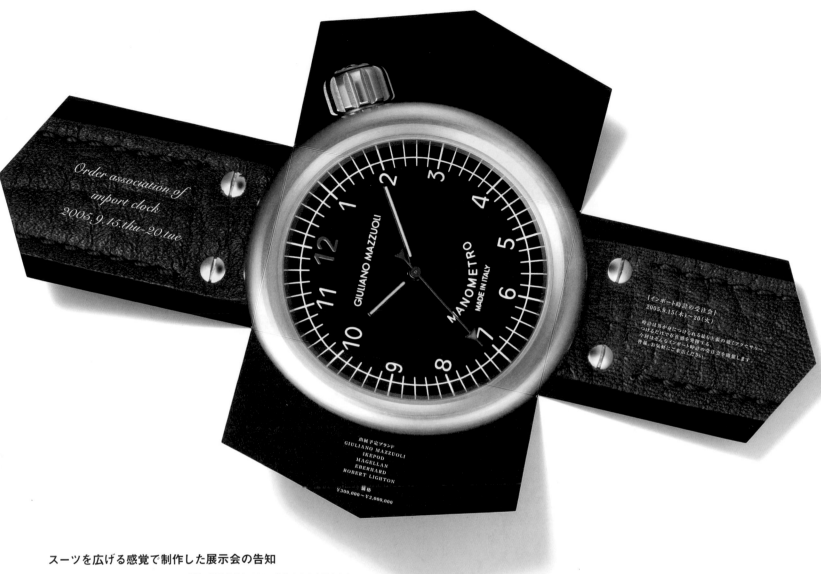

スーツを広げる感覚で制作した展示会の告知

ディテールにこだわりのあるスーツと時計の展示会告知DM。商品の良さを伝えられるよう、画像の映える印刷紙を選択。DMの折りはスーツを広げるイメージで生まれたアイデア。またコスト削減を考慮しDMと封筒を1枚で制作した結果、おもしろみのある形態に仕上げることができた。

The idea of unfolding a suit for notice of an exhibition

A DM notice for an exhibition of suits and watches known for their attention to detailing. Coated printing paper that would show the images to best effect was selected to convey the quality of the products. The idea stemmed from likening that the folds in the DM to unfolding a suit. To reduce costs, the DM and the envelope were produced as one unit in a fun and interesting way.

セレクトショップ / 展示会の招待状
Boutique / Fashion Show Invitation
CL：ビーアール ショップ B.R.SHOP　D：野本あや子 Ayako Nomoto
P：植野 淳 Jun Ueno　CW：仁田登基子 Tokiko Nitta　DF, SB：アトテーブル at-table

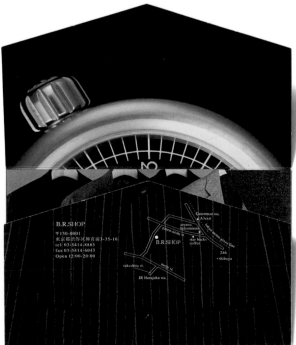

素材感のある演出で、新作発表を印象づけた
展示会招待状

ラグジュアリーで、デザイン性とクオリティの高いバッグやアクセサリーを提案する『KENJI IKEDA』の展示会招待状。高級感のあるレザーの質感を表現し、新作発表であることをアピールした。

Making an impression using the texture of new-release items for an invitation to an exhibition

An invitation to an exhibition by the Kenji Ikeda brand that offers luxury bags and accessories of high design and quality. The texture of the high-quality leather was expressed and that the bags were new releases was the appeal.

バッグ、アクセサリー / 展示会の招待状
Bag, Accessory / Fashion Show Invitation
CL：ケンジイケダ KENJI IKEDA Co., Ltd.   D：和田佳子 Yoshiko Wada
DF, SB：プロップ グラフィック ステーション PROP GRAPHIC STATION INC.

シリーズを通じ、統一したサイズで信頼感を与える展示会の招待状

ファッション性、機能性、先進性などを大切にした婦人靴を展開する『SHIN-EI』のコレクション招待状。2009年は、
シリーズを通して招待状を同じサイズで制作し、統一感のあるものに。

An invitation to an exhibition that inspires confidence with consistent sizing throughout the series

Shin-ei is the lady's shoes brand which make much of extreme, function, and fashionable look. The invitations for the
2009 collections were produced in the same size to create a sense of consistency.

靴の製造・販売 / 展示会の招待状　Footwear Manufacture and Sale / Fashion Show Invitation
CL：シンエイ　SHIN-EI Corporation　D：吉田望絵　Moe Yoshida
DF, SB：プロップ グラフィック ステーション　PROP GRAPHIC STATION INC.

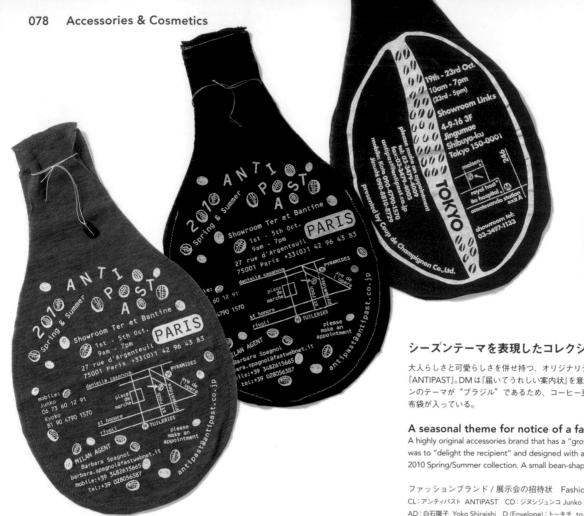

シーズンテーマを表現したコレクションの案内状

大人らしさと可愛らしさを併せ持つ、オリジナリティ溢れるソックス・洋服・小物を展開するブランド『ANTIPAST』。DMは『届いてうれしい案内状』を意識して作成。『2010 SPRING & SUMMER』コレクションのテーマが"ブラジル"であるため、コーヒー豆をモチーフにデザイン。封筒の中には豆型の小さな布袋が入っている。

A seasonal theme for notice of a fashion collection

A highly original accessories brand that has a "grown-up" sensibility but is also cute. The aim of the DM was to "delight the recipient" and designed with a coffee bean motif in line with the Brazil theme of the 2010 Spring/Summer collection. A small bean-shaped cloth bag was enclosed in the envelope also.

ファッションブランド / 展示会の招待状　Fashion Brand / Collection Invitation
CL：アンティパスト ANTIPAST　CD：ジヌシジュンコ Junko Jinushi / カトウキョウコ Kyoko Kato
AD：白石陽子 Yoko Shiraishi　D (Envelope)：トーキチ to-kichi
SB：クープ・ドゥ・シャンピニオン Coup de Champignon co., ltd.

オリジナルバッグの新登場を伝え、来店を促すDM

DMとしてだけでなく、ショップのウィンドウビジュアルとしても使用。オリジナルバッグの新登場を伝えるため、ストレートにバッグの形をしたカードに。『空押し』加工の特性を最大限に活かせる用紙を選び、押し加工で生まれる凸凹を利用してバッグの縫い目を再現。透明な封筒に入れて、手元に届いたときのインパクトを狙った。

A DM that conveys the debut of an original bag and connects to an increase in visitors to the store

A DM used not only as a DM but also as a visual for the window of the store. To convey the debuting of the original bag, a card in the shape of the bag was produced. A paper that was capable of maximizing the special features of blind embossing was selected, and the stitching on the bag was recreated using the raised surface created by the embossing process. The DM was placed in a transparent envelope to increase impact at the time of delivery.

アパレル / 新商品の案内状
Apparel / New Merchandise Announcement
CL, AD, D, SB：トゥモローランド TOMORROWLAND Co., Ltd.

SPECIAL INVITATION

SPECIAL KEY

TATSUMI-PLANNING

マンションをモチーフにした
リフォーム物件の展示会案内

マンション型のDMを開くと、室内が現れるようデザイン。展示会はマンションの一室で開催されるため、その部屋に訪れるときの疑似体験ができるように工夫した。付属の鍵を持って行くとプレゼントと交換できる。

Announcement for an exhibition renovated properties with an apartment as a motif

When the DM in the shape of an apartment is unfolded, the interior of the apartment appears. As the exhibition was held in a room in an apartment, the DM was devised to simulate the experience of visiting that room. The key that came with the DM could be exchanged for a present at the exhibition venue.

建築 / イベントの告知
Architecture / Event Announcement
CL：タツミプランニング　tatsumi planning
DF, SB：セルディビジョン　CELL DIVISION

リフォーム展示会開催！
リフォーム相談会も同時開催致します！
3月31日(土)・4月1日(日)

実際にリフォームした家をそのまま皆様に見て頂くために、リフォーム済みの物件を公開し、その場でリフォームの相談会を開催します。今回リフォームを手がけたのは、TVチャンピオンになったことでもお馴染みの清田直美。
お客様に合ったリフォームを提案します。
是非この機会にお気軽にお立ち寄り下さい。

これからリフォームをお考えの方、興味のある方
どなたでもお気軽にお越し下さい。

🎁 特典PRESENT!!
当日付属の鍵をお持ち頂いた方には
オリジナルフェイスタオル・ソープ
セットを先着40名様に差し上げます。
※アンケートにご記入頂いた方に限ります。

■開催日時・開催地
11:00am - 5:00pm
横浜市港北区樽町2-12-35
ライオンズマンション綱島第一301

お問い合わせ電話番号
045-228-1227
080-3481-0876
株式会社タツミプランニング
www.tatsumi-planning.co.jp

TVチャンピオン優勝の
清田直美が手がける
理想の部屋。

61.60㎡ 3DK→1LDK
オープンハウスとしてお客様に迫まってもらえるように、設備機器、水回りにもこだわりを体感してもらえる空間に。IHを使った料理教室やワインセミナーなど、パーティーイベントスペースにも。

清田 直美　Naomi Kiyota
TVチャンピオン第4回
「インテリアコーディネート王選手権」優勝
デザイナーズスタジオ 株式会社 代表
専門学校カレッジオブアーツ卒業後、インテリアデザイナーとして活躍。戸建住宅やマンションのモデルルーム及び個人住宅のデザインに携わる。TV・雑誌にも作品が取り上げられインテリアセミナー等も多数開催。

新たなる躍進への意志を
ストレートに伝えた挨拶状

創立60周年を迎える海運事業会社が国内外に送付したインビテーションとクリスマスカード。60→61への新たなる伝統と革新を訴求するデザインを目指した。中面は、『60』を厚盛りシルクで印刷し、『1』の数字とともに役員のサインを並べている。

A greeting card directly conveying an intention to go in new directions

An invitation and Christmas card sent within Japan and overseas by a marine transportation company that has been around for 60 years. The aim of the design was to appeal with the idea of new traditions and innovation from 60 to 61. On the inside, the 60 was printed with a raised silk printing process and together with the numeral 1, lists the signatures of company executives.

海運事業 / 季節の挨拶状
Marine Transportation / Seasonal Greetings
CL：インターオーシャン INTEROCEAN Co., Ltd.　CD, AD, D：渡辺雅之
Masayuki Watanabe　DF, SB：ティッドビット　Tidbit Co., Ltd.

a

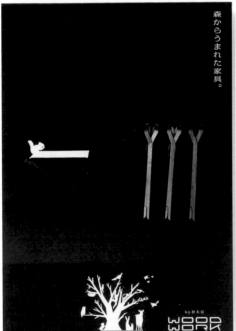

b

居心地のよい家具づくりへの
想いをカタチにしたDM

創業明治三十年の歴史を持つ材木屋が手掛ける家具ブランド『ウッドワーク』。新商品の案内(a)はシンプルに商品の魅力を訴求し、購入者へのお礼状(b)には店舗の看板犬を登場させた。店舗のオープン案内(c)は、コンセプトと商品を5枚のカードに分けて制作。親しみを持ってもらえるよう、飾れる美しいポストカード仕様に。

A DM based around the idea of making comfortable furniture

The furniture brand Woodwork operated by a timber dealer that has been around for more than 110 years. The information on products and sales (a) marketed the desirability of the products in a simple way. The store's mascot dog made an appearance in the thank-you letter to customers (b). The store-opening announcement (c) divided the concept and the products into five different cards. To convey a sense of friendliness, the specification was beautiful postcards that could displayed.

家具ブランド /
新商品の案内状、季節の挨拶状、店舗のオープン案内
Furniture Brand / New Merchandise Announcement, Seasonal Greetings, Opening Announcement
CL：ウッドワーク WOOD WORK   CD, AD, D, P：関 宙明 Hiroaki Seki
DF, SB：ミスター・ユニバース mr.universe

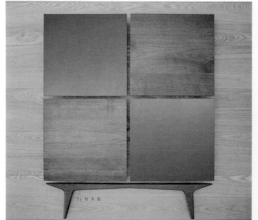

c

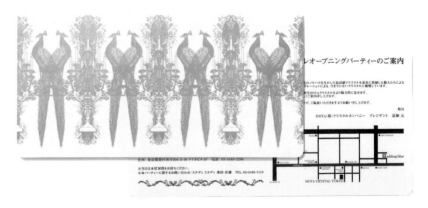

繊細なイラストが目を惹く内覧会＆パーティの案内状

光学ガラスの専門メーカーのショップ内覧会＆プレオープニングパーティの案内
状として制作したDMでは、繊細なイラストをメインに、箔押しUV加工でブラ
ンドイメージを伝えられるようにした。

Notice of a preview and party using a subtle illustration that catches the eye

The company has developed its business into a broad range of areas as a specialist
manufacturer of optical glass. The DM produced to give notice of a shop preview
and a pre-opening party conveys the brand image using a subtle illustration as a
key image, leaf and UV processing.

光学ガラスの専門メーカーのクリスタル事業 /
ショップ内覧会＆プレオープニングパーティの案内状
Optical Glassmaker's Crystal Business /
Notice of Shop Preview and Pre-opening Party
CL：HOYA クリスタルカンパニー　HOYA CORPORATION
CD, Planner：勢井浩二郎（デキスギ）Kojiro Sei（DEKISUGI）
AD, D, DF：伊藤桂司（UFG）Keiji Ito（UFG）　SB：デキスギ　DEKISUGI CORPORATION

シークレットパーティの扉を開く鍵を同封した招待状

外部デザイナーとのコラボレートブランド『TAKUMI（タクミ）』のシークレットクリスマスパーティの招待状。『シークレット』であるため、開催内容を隠すように赤い小箱に鍵とともに同封。グラフィックスに合わせてスワロフスキーを付けた台紙とともに透明なパッケージに入れ、パーティへの参加意欲を高めた。

An invitation containing a key that opens the door to a secret party

An invitation to a secret Christmas party held by TAKUMI, a brand that collaborates with outside designers. As the party is a "secret", the invitation is enclosed in a small red box to conceal the details, along with a key. To complement the graphics, the box has been placed inside transparent packaging on a Swarovski crystal base to heighten the desirability if the invitation.

ライフスタイルメーカー / シークレットパーティ招待状
Lifestyle Goods Manufacturer / Invitation to a Secret Party
CL, SB：イデアインターナショナル IDEA INTERNATIONAL CO., LTD.
CD, AD, D：たかはしるみ Rumi Takahashi

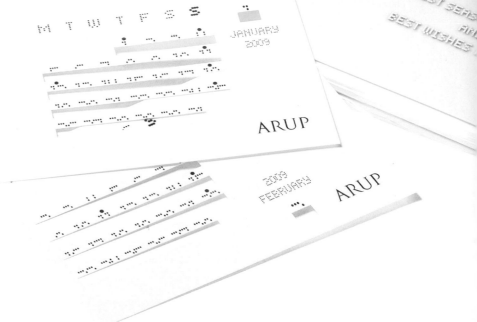

カレンダーが浮かび上がるよう工夫した
グリーティングカード

月毎に12枚のカードを用意。表面に各カードをのせると、その月のカレンダーに必要な情報だけがスリットから見えるため、カレンダーが浮かび上がってくるような印象に。文字はドット柄のフォントを使い、カードをのせる前の表面が何を意味するのかわからないよう工夫。カレンダーが浮かび上がったときの印象を大切にした。

A greeting card designed with a floating calendar

Twelve cards, one for every month of the year, were prepared. As only the information required for the calendar in a particular month is visible when the card for that month is at the front, the calendar appeared to be floating. A dot pattern font has been used for the text and designed so that the meaning only becomes clear once set in the proper position. Special consideration was given to the impression created by the floating calendar.

建築技術設計、コンサルティング / 季節の挨拶状
Construction Technology Design and Consulting / Seasonal Greetings
CL, SB：アラップ ジャパン Arup Japan   CD, AD, D：勝本恵子 Keiko Katsumoto

カレンダー機能を付けた顧客用のグリーティングカード

例年、年末に送る顧客宛の挨拶状にはカレンダー機能を付けている。郵送可能な筒状の透明ケースに収めた1枚のロール紙に12カ月分のカレンダーを印刷。各月はミシン目で切り離すことができ、最初と最後にはミニメッセージを印刷した。職種と関連付け、設計事務所で使うスケッチ紙をイメージし、手書き風のフォントを使用。

A greeting card for clients that has an additional calendar function

A calendar function was added to the greeting card usually sent to clients at the end of the year. The 12-month calendar printed on one sheet of paper was rolled up and inserted into a transparent tube ready for posting. The months of the year could be torn off along the perforated line and the top and bottom of the calendar was printed with a mini-message. A sketching paper image was used to connect to the company's business and a font in a hand-drawn style was used.

建築技術設計、コンサルティング / 季節の挨拶状
Construction Technology Design and Consulting / Seasonal Greetings
CL, SB：アラップ ジャパン Arup Japan   CD, AD, D：勝本恵子 Keiko Katsumoto

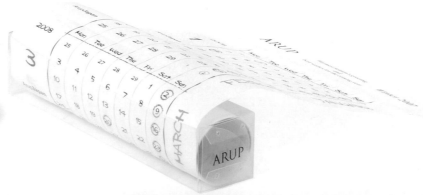

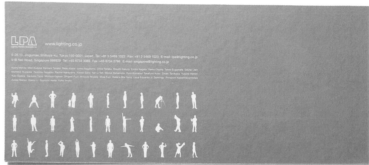
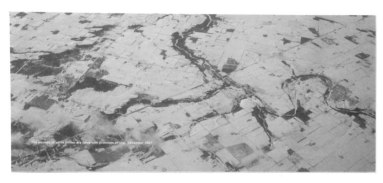

写真から感じる光の質感を活かした季節の挨拶状

照明計画や光のデザインなど、光環境の創出を提案する会社の季節の挨拶状。写真の季節感を活かすよう、色遣いや
印刷加工を工夫して質感を表現。会社が持つ大人らしさがうまく伝わるよう、落ち着いたトーンでまとめた。

A seasonal greeting card that uses the texture of the light perceptible in photographs

A seasonal greeting card from a company that offers creation of "light environments" that includes lighting planning
and light design. To maximize the seasonal aspect of the photographs, texture was expressed with specially devised
color schemes and printing processes. So as to properly convey the sophisticated image of the company, the design
was brought together with understated tones.

照明計画、デザイン、コンサルティング、研究・開発デザイン / 季節の挨拶状
Lighting Planning and Design, Consulting, Research, Development Design / Seasonal Greetings
CL：ライティング プランナーズ アソシエーツ Lighting Planners Associates Inc.
AD, D：金曽寛太 Kanta Kaneso   SB：エレダイ eredie Ltd.

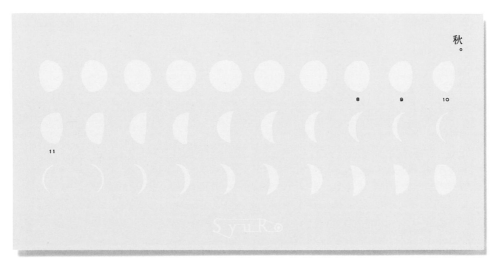

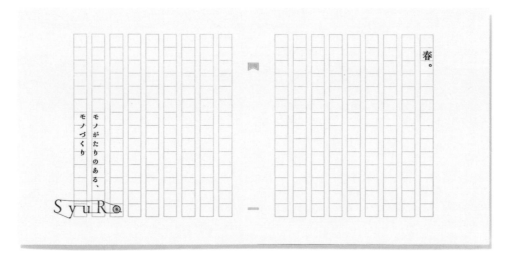

活版印刷で温もりのあるモノづくりを表現した展示会の招待状

体温を感じるデザインで、素材の心地良さを大切にしたモノづくりを続ける生活デザイン雑貨店『SyuRo』が、
定期的に行う『モノがたりのある、モノづくり展』の招待状。活版印刷を用い、その時期の新商品に合わせたビ
ジュアルで新鮮な訴求を心がけている。

An invitation to an exhibition that expresses with letterpress printing the joy of making things

An invitation using a warm design to the "Monogatari no aru Monozukuriten" held regularly by the life-style design store SyuRo that values the quality of the materials from which its things are made. The aim was a fresh approach to marketing its products using letterpress printing and visuals that matched the products available at the time.

雑貨の製作販売・卸 / 展示会の招待状
Production, Sale, Wholesale of Miscellaneous Goods / Exhibition Invitation

CL：シュロ SyuRo　CD, AD, D：関 宙明　Hiroaki Seki　DF, SB：ミスター・ユニバース　mr.universe

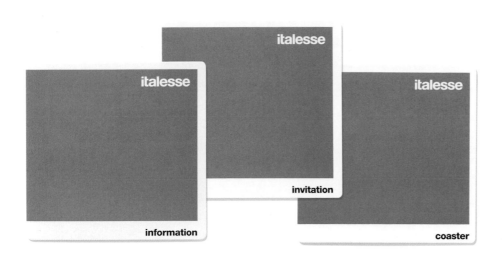

2009/6/11 invitation

洗練されたデザインのコースター仕立てにした展示会の招待状

ワイングラスなど、洗練されたデザインや機能性で、クオリティの高いアイテムを展開するイタリアン・ブランド『italesse』の展示会招待状。テーブルウェアのブランドであるため、招待状自体をコースター仕様にした。

An invitation to an exhibition with a sophisticated design presented in the form of coaster

An invitation to an exhibition of the Italian brand italesse that offers high-quality items such as wine glasses with a sophisticated design as well as functionality. As it is a tableware brand, the invitation was presented in the form of coaster.

テーブルウェア / 展示会の招待状
Tableware / Fashion Show Invitation
CL：レイジースーザン LAZY SUSAN Co., Ltd. / イタレッセ italesse　D：吉田望絵 Moe Yoshida
DF, SB：プロップ グラフィック ステーション PROP GRAPHIC STATION INC.　Agency：ハウ HOW INCORPORATED

老舗家具ショップが発信する顧客への購入後の案内

家具の里のコンセプトである『暮らしになじむ家族家具』をベースに、かわいく、わかりやすくかつ安心感を伝えられるデザインとした。付録のメジャーや封筒の中面に隠れキャラを印刷するなど、ちょっとした遊び心も加えられている。

After-sales information provided to valued customers of a long-established furniture store

The design, based on Kagunosato's concept of "family furniture that becomes a part of your lifestyle," is cute, accessible and imparts a sense of comfort. A sense of fun has also been added by the complimentary tape measure and the concealed character printed on the inside of the envelope.

家具販売 / 購入後の案内　Furniture Retailer / After-sales Information
CL：家具の里 kagu no sato　AD, D, Logo Design：三島優樹 Yuki Mishima　Logo Design：高見祐介 Yusuke Takami
I：矢立 恭 Kyo Yatate　DF, SB：ソララ Solala co., ltd.

カラフルな色遣いでテーマの愉しさを伝えるプレスリリース

『Afternoon Tea LIVING』では、28周年を記念して『Life with Colors』をテーマに商品を展開。『生活の中にカラーを加え、日々の生活を愉しく』というコンセプトであるため、愉しいリビングシーンをコラージュで表現。ページ毎にカラフルな色をプラスし、色の楽しさを演出した。

A press release conveying the pleasure of the theme with a vivid color scheme

At Afternoon Tea LIVING, products were developed with the theme of Life with Colors to celebrate the 28th anniversary. As the concept was "Add color to brighten up everyday life," fun lifestyle scenes were expressed using collages. Vivid colors were added to each page to highlight the pleasure of color.

リビング雑貨小売業 / イベントの告知、新商品の案内状
Miscellaneous Lifestyle Goods Production and Retail Sales /
Event Announcement, New Merchandise Announcement
CL, SB：アイシーエル ICL Inc.　D：野元 陽 Yo Nomoto　P：堂園康仁 Yasuhito Dozono
CW：松浦 祐 Yutaka Matsuura　Collage：有賀さおり Saori Ariga

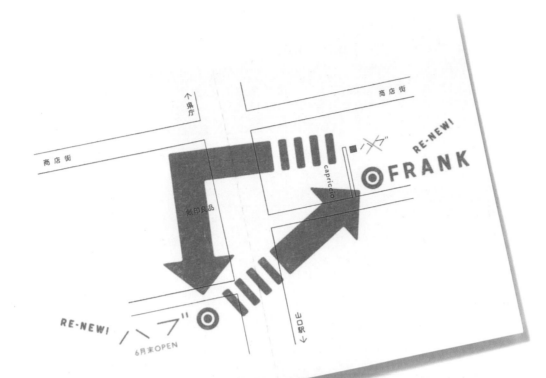

姉妹店である2店舗の場所を地図で
見せたユニークな移転案内

姉妹店の移転告知を図解で説明。ミシン目を切り離す
と各店舗のショップカードになる。

**A unique change of premises notice
that shows a map of the location of
two affiliated stores**

The change of premises notice for two affiliated stores
has been explained in diagram format. Tear along the
perforation and you have a shop card for each store.

食材＆雑貨、カフェ＆バー／移転案内
Grocery & Sundry Goods, Cafe & Bar /
Moving Announcement
CL, CD：フランク FRANK / ハブ Hub
AD, D：野村勝久 Katsuhisa Nomura
D：神 大樹 Taiju Kami
CW：大賀郁子 Ikuko Oga
DF, SB：野村デザイン制作室 NOMURA DESIGN FACTORY

食材＆雑貨のお店として ニューオープン

カフェFARNKで用いてきた厳選した食材や、職人の手仕事による雑貨など、作り手の心がこもった商品を扱うショップになります。小さなカフェスペースも備えた、新スタイルのFRANKにご期待ください。

FRANKとハブが生まれ変わります

FRANK
〒753-0087 山口市米屋町2-26
TEL.083-932-4836
営業時間 11:00-20:00　定休日 火曜日

カフェ＆バーとして ニューオープン

にぎやかな駅通りに移り、夜にお酒を味わう小さなお店から、ランチやお茶も楽しめる広いお店に転身。FRANKプロデュースで、お昼はカフェ、夜はバーの顔をもつ、新たなハブの歩みがはじまります。

ハブ
〒753-0047 山口市道場門前2-4-19-2F
TEL.080-3053-6599
営業時間 12:00-27:00　定休日 火曜日

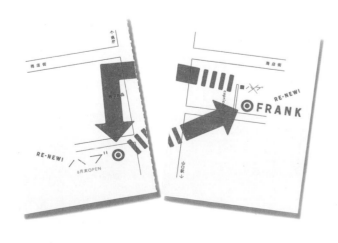

a

b

営業スケジュールも兼ねた季節の挨拶状

フランスの有名店で修行を積んだオーナーシェフの繊細な料理が定評な高級フレンチレストラン。冬の挨拶状 (a) では箔押ししたテーブルセットを型抜きにし、高級感とお落ち着き感あるモダンなデザインにした。夏の挨拶状 (b) では特殊紙と銀箔押しで清涼感を演出。

A seasonal greeting card that also serves as a business schedule

A high-quality French restaurant that serves beautiful cuisine prepared by the owner chef who learnt his craft in famous French restaurants. The modern design of the winter greeting card (a) was of a high quality and understated using foil and a cutout of a table setting. For the summer greeting card (b), special paper and silver foil were used for a fresh look.

フレンチレストラン / 季節の挨拶状
French Restaurant / Seasonal Greetings
CL：ラ・ベカス La Bécasse　AD：真木克英 Katsuhide Maki　D：牧田康平 Kohei Makita
DF, SB：アレックスクリエイト alexcreate co., ltd.

幻想的な氷の世界を演出した移転案内状

壁やバーカウンター、テーブルや彫刻にいたるまで氷でできている『アイスバー東京』。同店のイメージが伝わる
ようにフェイクの氷を真空パック加工し、ホログラム紙で幻想的な氷の世界を演出した。

Change of premises notice that creates a fantasy world of ice

ICEBAR TOKYO where the walls, the bar counter, the tables and sculpture are all made of ice. To convey the bar's
image, fake ice was put through a vacuum-packing process and hologram paper used to create a fantasy world of ice.

バー / 移転案内　Bar / Moving Announcement
CL：アイスバー東京 ICEBAR TOKYO　CD：浅尾浩一 Koichi Asao　AD, D：山崎弘幸 Hiroyuki Yamazaki
DF, SB：ノーザングラフィックス Northern Graphics

自然な優しさやヘルシーさを表現したパーティ招待状

オーガニックフードのセレクトショップ『シナグロ』のオープニングパーティ招待状。オーガニックを連想させ
る優しい色や紙を採用し、箔押しでさりげなくロゴを配した。

A party invitation expresses a natural gentleness and healthiness

An invitation to a party for the opening of the organic food select shop, Cinagro. Soft colors and paper that
suggested the idea of organic were used and the foil logo casually arranged.

オーガニックフードのセレクトショップ / オープニングパーティの招待状
Organic Food Select Shop / Opening Party Invitation
CL：薬糧開発　Yakuryokaihatsu.co., ltd　AD, D, SB：グルーヴィジョンズ　groovisions

顧客への満足度を高める『旬の会』入会後の案内

『旬の会』に入会いただいた顧客の満足度を高めるために制作。コンセプトである『旬シリーズは自然の贈りもの』を、写真をメインビジュアルにし伝えた。入会者特典のかわいいトマト柄のオリジナル手ぬぐいも同封されている。

Notice sent to new members of Shun no Kai (Season Club) to increase customer satisfaction

Produced with the aim of increasing the satisfaction level of customers who had become members of the Shun no Kai (Season Club). The concept of "the seasonal series is one of nature's gifts" was conveyed via the main visual. A special gift of an original hand towel in a cute tomato pattern was also enclosed.

食料品 /『旬の会』入会後の案内
Food Products / Notice Sent to New Members of Shun no Kai (Season Club)
CL, SB：カゴメ　KAGOME CO., LTD.　CD, AD：藤井康成　Yasunari Fujii　D：田辺太一　Taichi Tanabe / 伊藤 梢　Kozue Ito
P：永井秀和　Hidekazu Nagai　CW：柚木めぐみ　Megumi Yunoki　DF：博報堂プロダクツ　HAKUHODO PRODUCT'S

質感の変化で好奇心を喚起させるベルギービール専門店の開店案内

ベルギービールグラス特有の型にすることで、ベルギービール専門店であることをアピール。手にしたとき、触感を楽しむと同時に好奇心がそそられるよう、密かに質感に変化を加えた。泡の部分には弾力のある特殊な紙を使用し、ビールのきめ細かさを表現。パーティー案内とクーポンをビールキャップ型にし、特別感を演出した。

Information on the opening of a store specializing in Belgian beer that arouses the curiosity with variations of texture

The Belgian beer specialty store was marketed with a model of the unique Belgian beer glass. Changes were discreetly added to the texture so that curiosity was aroused as the tactile sense was stimulated when the glass was picked up. A special flexible paper was used for the foam to express the delicacy of the grain of the beer. Information on the party and a coupon were made into the shape of a beer cap to create a special feeling.

ベルギービール専門店 / オープンの告知   Store Specializing in Belgian Beer / Opening Announcement
CL, SB：ダイヤモンドダイニング Diamond Dining Co., Ltd.

ビールの豊富な品揃えをアピールした
ビアカフェのオープン案内

ベルギービールをはじめ、世界各国のビールを扱う店であるため、各ビールの銘柄のロゴを一面に配置し、豊富な品揃えをアピールした。ビールのコースターをイメージし、厚みを出すため3枚の紙を合紙。表面にはコースターのざらついた質感に近い紙を選んだ。

Opening announcement of a beer cafe that appeals with its abundant range of beers

As the beer cafe deals in beers from various countries including Belgium, the logos for each brand of beer were placed on the front page, making an appeal with the large stock of different beers available. Three sheets of paper joined together were used to add thickness to the DM that had the image of a beer coaster. A paper that was close in terms of texture to a beer coaster was used for the top layer.

ビアカフェ / オープンの告知
Beer Cafe / Opening Announcement
CL, SB：ダイヤモンドダイニング Diamond Dining Co., Ltd.

不思議の国のアリスをモチーフにしたレストランの
オープン案内

メインモチーフには大きなウサギを起用し、DMが届いたときの"驚き"と店への"期待"をメインに考えて制作。"絵本"の世界にスポットを当てた店であるため、中紙の表面にはアリス独特の世界を表現。ゴールドの紙を使うことで高級感を出し、細かい部分に様々な加工をすることでコンセプトであるゴシック感を演出した。

Restaurant-opening announcement with an Alice in Wonderland motif
The DM was produced using a large rabbit as a main motif and with the idea of creating "surprise" and "anticipation" for the restaurant when the DM was delivered. As the restaurant is based around a picture book, the special world of Alice was expressed on the inside pages. A sense of quality was produced using gold paper and a Gothic atmosphere by applying various processes to detailed areas of the DM.

レストラン／オープンの告知　Restaurant / Opening Announcement
CL, SB：ダイヤモンドダイニング　Diamond Dining Co., Ltd.

ラグジュアリーなダイニングが開催する8周年のイベント案内

『大人たちが夜を浮遊する大陸』を形にしたダイニング＆ラウンジが、8周年を迎えるにあたってイベントを開催。告知フライヤーでは、クリスマスのイメージに加え、8周年の華やかさをホログラムの箔押しで表現した。

Notice of event to celebrate eight years of luxury dining

An event held to celebrate the eighth year of a restaurant and lounge described as a "continent where grown-ups float across the night." The notice expressed the gaiety of the milestone using a hologram in gold foil in addition to a Christmas image.

ダイニング＆ラウンジ /
イベントの告知、8周年フライヤー
Dining & Lounge /
Event Announcement, Flyer for the Eighth Anniversary
CL：アフリカ代官山 Africa Daikanyama
AD, D：小島里沙 Lisa Kojima
P：川上陽子 Yoko Kawakami
SB：オペレーションファクトリー Operation Factory

全国各地のこだわりの酒を扱うセレクトショップの開店案内

全国から集めたこだわりの日本酒や焼酎を扱う酒店『SAKE Atelier』の開店告知。ロゴはセレクトショップの酒屋らしいデザインにし、イラストは建築デザイナーが描いたものに。

Announcement for the opening of a boutique sake store that deals in sake from around Japan.

An opening of the boutique sake store, Sake Atelier that deals in sake and shochu from around Japan. The logo had a typical boutique sake store design and the illustrations were drawn by an architectural designer.

酒のセレクトショップ / オープンの告知
Boutique Sake Store / Opening Announcement
CL：越前酒乃店はやし Echizen Sakenomise Hayashi
AD, D：中野勝巳 Katsumi Nakanao
DF, SB：中野勝巳デザイン室 Nakano design

銀をベースにダイレクトに展開した
オープニングパーティの招待状

お酒を愛する大人の為のレストラン『Ag』のオープニングパーティ招待状。
店名は銀の元素記号からつけられ、コンセプトは食をきっかけに輝くライフ
スタイルを提案すること。同店のコンセプトを銀色をベースにダイレクトに
展開した。

A base of silver for an invitation to an opening party

An invitation to a party for the opening of the Ag restaurant for connoisseurs
of sake. The restaurant's name was taken from the chemical element of silver
and the concept was to offer a glamorous lifestyle through dining. A base of
silver was used to develop the concept of the restaurant in a straightforward
way.

レストラン / オープニングパーティの招待状
Restaurant / Opening Party Invitation
CL：アナログ　ANALOG　AD：相澤幸彦　Yukihiko Aizawa
D：永田千奈　China Nagata　DF, SB：相澤事務所　aizawa office

パールやトレペの加工紙を使い、
高級感と遊びを一体化させたDM

バー・ラウンジ『アン・ヴォーグ』の7周年DM。高級感を出すため、本体にはキュリアスメタルを使用。挨拶状は、キュリアスTL（カラートレペ）にロゴと『7』のローマ数字を組み合わせてアイキャッチとして展開し、重ねて見せる遊びも取り入れた。

A DM that unifies a sense of quality and fun using pearl and tracing processed paper

A DM for the seven-year anniversary of the en. Vogue bar and lounge. To convey a sense of quality, curious metal was used in the main body of the DM. For the greeting card, the logo and the number for 7 were combined on Curious TL (colored tracing paper) and developed to be eye-catching, incorporating the fun of superimposed images.

バー・ラウンジ／7周年のDM
Bar and lounge / DM for Seven-year Anniversary
CL：アン・ヴォーグ en.Vogue　AD, D：中野勝巳 Katsumi Nakanao　D：石田美和 Miwa Ishida
CW：黒田和彦 Kazuhiko Kuroda　DF, SB：中野勝巳デザイン室 Nakano design
DF：シーディーアイ CDI

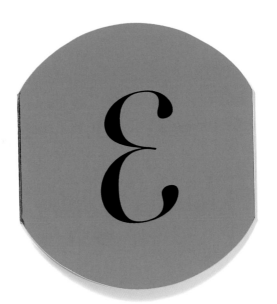

おかげさまで
KOMACHIは
3周年を迎える事が
出来ました。

皆様のご愛顧に
感謝申し上げます。

佐々木香代
スタッフ一同

3周年の『3』をストレートに
表現した告知DM

バー・ラウンジ『KOMACHI』の3周年記念のサービス案内。三面鏡をコンセプトに、少しゆがんだ数字の『3』をミラー系の紙に印刷した。

**Third-anniversary announcement
that expresses 3 in a direct way**
Information on the complimentary service for the third anniversary of the Komachi bar and lounge. Based on the concept of a three-panel mirror, a slightly distorted number 3 was printed with mirror-coated paper.

おかげさまで
KOMACHIは
3周年を迎える事が
出来ました。

皆様のご愛顧に
感謝申し上げます。

佐々木香代
スタッフ一同

Thanks the 3rd.
Special 3 Days.
8/20thu.〜22sat.

いつもご愛顧ありがとうございます。
3周年の感謝の気持ちを込めたスペシャルな
3日間をご用意いたしました。
スタッフ一同、皆様のご来店をお待ちいたしております。

バー・ラウンジ / 3周年のDM
Bar and Lounge / DM for Third Anniversary
CL：コマチ KOMACHI
AD, D：中野勝巳 Katsumi Nakanao
CW：小笠道睦 Douboku Ogasa
DF, SB：中野勝巳デザイン室 Nakano design
DF：シュガーポット Sugarpot

洒落た大人の雰囲気でまとめた
オープニングパーティの招待状

落ち着いた大人の雰囲気でお酒と料理が楽しめる能阿のオープニングパーティ用DM。お店のイメージを大切にシンプルにまとめた。1ドリンクサービスのうれしい特典つき。

**A stylish "grown-up" look for an invitation to
an opening party**
A DM for the opening party at Noa, a restaurant where food and beverages can be enjoyed in an understated grown-up atmosphere. The restaurant's image has been expressed in a simple and careful manner. A coupon for one free drink was attached.

飲食店 / オープニングパーティの招待状
Restaurant / Opening Party Invitation
CL：能阿 Noa   AD：池田享史 Takafumi Ikeda
D：高尾元樹 Motoki Takao / 戸金珠美 Tamami Togane / 川内栄子 Eiko Kawauchi
SB：デザインサービス design service inc.

1 drink service
(champagne)

『旅館』をコンセプトとした複合飲食店の開店案内

コンセプトが『旅館に併設された別邸の食事処』であるため、旅館をイメージさせる粗品の『てぬぐい』をオリジナルデザインで制作し、同封。4種類の店舗が入った複合飲食店であることから、パンフレットでは各店の案内を見出しごとに分け、すべて広げると入り口のファサードが大きく登場するよう、折り方にこだわった。

Opening announcement for a restaurant complex with the concept of a Japanese inn

As the concept is "an eatery in a villa annexed to a Japanese inn," a small gift of a tenugui towel that conjured up the image of a Japanese-style inn was produced in an original design and enclosed with the DM. As there were four types of business inside the restaurant complex, the information in the pamphlet about each business was divided under four headings and special consideration was given to the way the DM was folded so that when each was opened out, the facade of its entranceway appeared in large form.

飲食店 / オープンの告知　Restaurant / Opening Announcement
CL, SB：ダイヤモンドダイニング　Diamond Dining Co., Ltd.

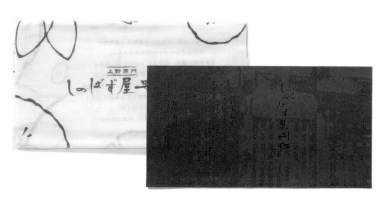

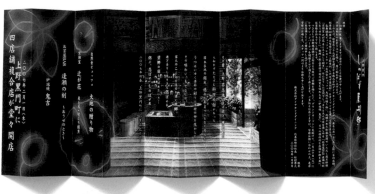

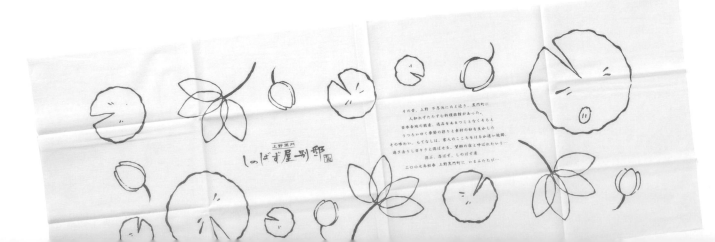

空の巻⋯空の巻とは

その壱　場の空間真を読む空気感の大切さについて説いたものなり

その弐　上司と囲むは⋯まずは相手の出方をうかがいみるべし

その参　部下と囲むは⋯光家を旅し

その四　想いの人と⋯鍋をつつけば⋯その壱　一歩前進

その伍　もてなしの前は⋯まず　財布の中身を確認（空にするべからず）

風の巻⋯風の巻とは

その壱　地を語る　その鍋　器自慢の奥ゆかしく

その弐　盛りつけに　一宇あり　目に美味し

その参⋯大和魂に宿る鍋の心　風流について説いたものなり

火の巻⋯火の巻とは

その壱　御座なりにされがちな火力　火力調の大切さについて説いたものなり

その弐　がちがちゃと⋯火を始めるのが鍋奉行　びびっとさげない

その参　悪い習慣　越めの温泉　水面を保つべし

その四　決して　出汁を飛ばすべからず

水の巻⋯水の巻とは

その壱　肉は汁を⋯鍋出汁の大切さについて説いたものなり

その弐　肉は光、野菜は根なり⋯ことごとに⋯

その参　肉に肉あり　出汁にしてでた出汁

地の巻⋯地の巻とは

その壱　大地の恵みを全身全霊で喜ぶことについて説いたものなり

その弐　大地の恵みを　野菜の美味を　侮るべからず

その参　野菜の美味を⋯肉を知れば　百倍にして　喜びあり

その四　四季を愛し　旬を知れば　百倍にして　喜びあり

あくとり代官　鍋之進

鍋道 五輪の書

あくとり代官　鍋之進

目もくらむ程、美味い鍋

あくとり代官　鍋之進

10月19日（金）開店

株式会社ダイヤモンドダイニング　Diamond Dining

金色でコンセプトと祝いの意を表現した鍋専門店の開店案内

『目もくらむ程、美味い鍋』というキャッチコピーに合わせると当時に、50店舗目の出店という祝いの意も込め、金ピカの紙を使用。時代劇で悪代官に渡される賄賂（小判）や、祝いの席の金屏風を連想させる金色にこだわった。この紙で、挨拶の手紙、店舗案内、割引券と鍋のこだわりを謳った『鍋道 五輪の書』を包んでいる。

Opening announcement for a cooking pan specialty store that expresses the concept and desire to celebrate with gold

To go with the catch copy "a pan so delicious it will make you dizzy, " shiny gold paper was used to celebrate the opening of the fiftieth store. Special consideration was given to the fact that the gold color resembled the gold coins given to corrupt administrators as bribes in historical dramas and the gold folding screen in places of celebration. The paper was used to wrap the greeting, information on the store, a discount voucher and "The Way of the Pan: The Book of Five Rings, " a publication for all pan fanatics.

鍋専門店 / オープンの告知　Cooking Pan Specialty Store / Opening Announcement
CL, SB：ダイヤモンドダイニング　Diamond Dining Co., Ltd.

3 大感謝

3.3 ANNIVERSARY

炭火焼肉深山 中目黒

2004年10月の開店から早くも3周年を迎えることができました。
みなさまへの感謝をこめて、当店自慢のお肉をご用意させていただきました。（当店の人気メニュー）本日のリブロース（約150g）を大感謝サービスのお料理でのサービスとなります。
※お食事は人によってご用意できる場合とできない場合と両料クラスよろしくお願い致します。
※ご予約をおすすめしています。スムーズにご案内できますようお願いいたします。またこのDMにのせてのなにとぞ
またこのDMにのせてでないサービス
このDMを期間内に店舗にご持参していただきますので、このDMご持参ください※※

このサービスは2008年4月末までのサービスさせていただきます

炭火焼肉 深山
153-0051 東京都目黒区上目黒3-16-13
CUBE-M B1　Phone.03-5722-3805
OPEN：18:00-24:30 (火・日)
　　　 23:30 (LO)
CLOSE：月曜日

思わず店舗へ足を運びたくなるリアルな牛肉の形をしたDM

開店3周年を記念し送付したDM。捨てられない、忘れられないDMを目指し、形から手触りまで本物らしさにこだわり、白とピンクのゴム素材で制作。顧客の食欲にダイレクトに訴えかけた。このDMを期間内に店舗に持参すれば150gのリブロースがサービスされるといううれしい特典も集客数のアップに結びついた。

A DM that uses the shape of real beef to tempt customers to the restaurant

A DM sent out for the third anniversary of the opening of the restaurant. The aim was to create a DM that would not be simply discarded or forgotten. That the DM actually resembled real beef from the shape to the texture was important and therefore it was produced in layers of white and pink rubber, appealing directly to the appetite of the customer. The special offer of a free 150gm rib roast for customers who brought the DM to the restaurant within the period resulted in an increase in the number of customers.

焼肉店 / イベントの告知　Restaurant / Event Announcement
CL：焼肉深山 Miyama　SB：フルマークス FULLMARKS

ショップカードとしても使用できる1ショップ1シートの案内状

9カテゴリーのレンタルショップとWEB販売を行うファッションショップ・マナマナ。各ショップの特徴を表現するため、
それぞれの商品を使用しモチーフを制作。1ショップ1シート形式にすることで個別でも使用でき、また情報の刷新も容
易にできるという機能性にも優れた案内状となった。

A "one shop, one information sheet" that can also be used as a shop card

Fashion store mahna mahna is a rental store for nine categories of goods and an Internet retail store. To express the
individual character of each store, the information sheets were produced with a motif of their respective products. The "one
shop, one information sheet" format means that the sheets can be used individually and also be updated easily with new
information.

ファッションレンタル及び販売 / 会社＆ショップ案内状
Fashion Rental and Rental Sales / Company and Store Information
CL：マナマナ mahna mahna   AD：西谷圭介 Keisuke Nishitani   D：藤本 岳 Gaku Fujimoto / 福中聡顕 Akiteru Fukunaka
P：山根範久 Norihisa Yamane   DF, SB：スリーアンドコー Three & Co.   Stylist：天野恭子 Kyoko Amano

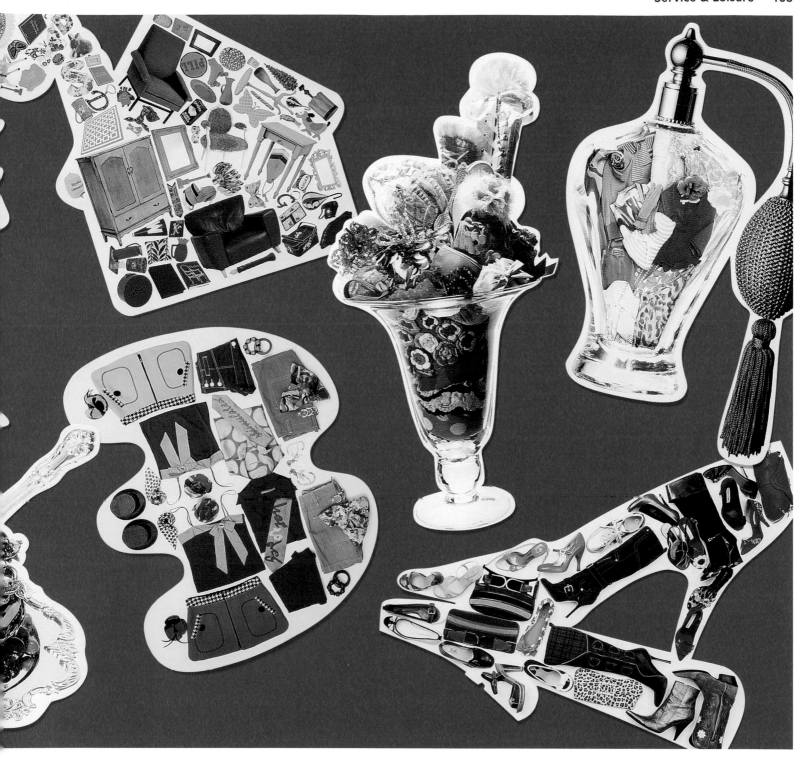

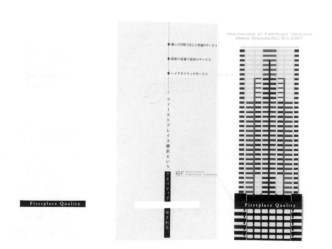

優雅な空間で健康をサポートする総合健診センターのオープン案内

健診センターを開設する新設ビル『ファーストプレイス横浜』の持つクオリティと、そこにオープンすることへの期待感をアピール。外観そのものをモチーフとして取り上げることで、具体的なイメージを見る側に与え、全体的にワンランク上のクオリティ・モダンさを感じさせるデザインに仕上げた。

Information on the opening of a general medical center that provides health services in elegant surroundings

The appeal was based on the quality of the new Firstplace Yokohama building in which the medical center was established and the sense of anticipation for the opening. By using an external view of the building as a motif, the viewer was given a concrete image of the medical center and the overall design conveyed a sense of the center's high quality and modernity.

医療 / 施設のオープン案内　Medical / Opening Announcement

CL：医療法人社団 善仁会 ZENJINKAI GROUP　DF, SB：セルディビジョン CELL DIVISION

CONTACT STUDIO ROOF 2009.6.1 OPEN!

フォトスタジオの
オープニングパーティ招待状

レンタル・フォトスタジオ『CONTACT STUDIO ROOF』のオープニングパーティ招待状。全体としてひとつのビルを連想できるよう写真を配置し、デザイン。スタジオの造りや雰囲気をわかりやすく伝えている。

An invitation to the opening of a photo studio

An invitation to the opening of the rental photo studio Contact Studio Roof. The design involves the placement of photographs that can be associated with the building as a whole. The structure and the atmosphere of the studio are clearly conveyed.

フォトスタジオ / オープニングパーティの招待状
Photo Studio / Opening Party Invitation
CL：コンタクト スタジオ ルーフ　CONTACT STUDIO ROOF
AD, D：カワムラヒデオ　Hideo Kawamura
SB：カワムラヒデオアクティビィティ　Kawamura Hideo Activity Inc.

見る人を旅へと誘う隠れ家的ホテルのオープン告知

見る人を旅へと誘うよう、表紙に設けられた四角い窓から瀬戸内海の青い海をのぞき見ることができるようにした。瀬戸内海の絶景を満喫できる贅沢な旅時間を、シンプルにまとめたデザインと物語調につづられた紹介文で表現している。

Notice of the opening of a "hideaway hotel" that tempts the viewer to go on holiday

Designed so that glimpses of the blue of the Seto Inland Sea can be seen through the square window in the cover and to tempt the viewer to go on holiday. The idea of taking a luxurious holiday enjoying superb views of the Seto Inland Sea has been expressed with a simple design and a "story-like" introductory text.

宿泊施設 / オープンの告知　Accommodation / Opening Announcement
CL：風の音舎　KAZENOOTO　AD, D：三島優樹　Yuki Mishima　DF, SB：ソララ　Solala co., ltd.

ヴィラ
風の音
VILLA KAZENOOTO

瀬戸内からの招待状。

これから、クルーザーに乗せてお連れするのは、瀬戸内海のほぼ真ん中に浮かぶ、
小さな楽園「豊島(としま)」。
いまだかつて体験したことのない非日常感。ゆったりした時間に身をゆだねる贅沢。
そこに建つ＜ヴィラ 風の音＞が、とびきりパーソナルで上質な旅の味わいを、
あなたにお約束いたします。

『サーカス』をテーマにしたネイルサロンの挨拶状

ネイルサロンの集客用として季節ごとに配布しているDMと、クリスマスに送付された顧客向けのThankyouカード。テーマである『サーカス』でわくわくするような期待感を与えつつ、ピンクと黒で女性らしいやわらかな雰囲気を醸し出した。

A greeting card for a nail salon featuring a "circus" theme

A DM distributed every season to increase customers to the nail salon and a Thank-You card sent to customers at Christmas time. The circus theme imparts an exciting sense of anticipation in addition to the soft, feminine look created in pink and black.

ネイルサロン / 季節の挨拶状
Nail Salon / Seasonal Greetings
CL：石田絞子 Ayako Ishida　AD, D：平原由紀子 Yukiko Hirahara　SB：ケイク　cake

人なつっこいロゴで『人を笑顔に』
10周年＆CI変更のお知らせ

10周年を機に、同社が大切にしてきた『知力・考える力』という企業テーマに『人間力・温かみ』という新たなテーマを加え、新しいロゴを作成。ユーモアで人なっこいロゴデザインには『人を笑顔にしたい』という想いが込められている。

Notice of the tenth year of making people smile and a change to the CI with a friendly logo

On the occasion of the tenth anniversary, a new logo was produced by adding the new theme of "human power/warmth" to the existing corporate theme valued by the company of "intellect/power to think." The idea of "making people smile" has been incorporated into the humorous and friendly logo design.

IT / 10周年＆CI変更のお知らせ
IT / Notice of Tenth Anniversary and Change of CI
CL：オロ ORO　CD, CW：小西利行　Toshiyuki Konishi
AD, D, I：金子 敦 Atsushi Kaneko　AD, D：金子泰子 Yasuko Kaneko
DF, SB：ブラッド チューブ インク　Blood Tube Inc.

タトゥーシールつき Halloween Party の招待状

coletteのニューアルバムリリースを記念して開催された Halloween Party の招待状。表面は仮装気分を盛り上げてくれる髭のタトゥーシール。髭の先をリボンにしたタイプや colette となっているものもあり、好みにあわせてチョイスできるようにした。

Invitation to a Halloween Party with tattoo sticker

An invitation to a Halloween Party held to celebrate the release of a new album by Colette. The front of the invitation is a beard tattoo to liven up the masquerade. You can choose your favorite, either the one where the ends of the beard are ribbons or the one of colette.

商業施設 / イベントの告知　Commercial Complex / Event Announcement
CL：colette　AD, D, I, SB：大島慶一郎 Keiichiro Oshima

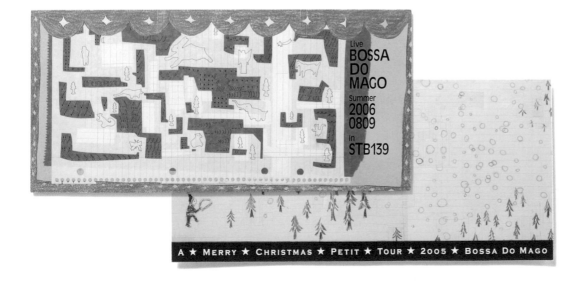

コラージュで多重的な音楽の世界観を表現したライブ告知DM

ライブ『BOSSA DO MAGO』の多重的な音楽を連想してもらえるよう、用紙をコラージュして画面を多層に。絵柄が繊細であるため、書体で締めた。

A DM giving notice of a live music event that expresses a worldview of multilayer music with collage

To create an association with the multilayer music of the live BOSSA DO MAGO event, sheets of paper were formed into collages with a multilayered picture plane. The intricate pattern was tied together with a typeface.

レコードレーベル / ライブ告知DM
Record Label / Notice of Live Music Event
CL：ナースレコーズ nuss records
AD, D, I：紀太みどり Midori Kida　DF, SB：タイニー tiny

カジノを舞台にした映画
『オーシャンズ13』のイベント告知

ラスベガスのカジノを舞台に繰り広げられる犯罪アクション『オーシャンズ13』。舞台となるカジノを連想させるゴージャスな雰囲気を全面に出しつつ、アルファベットをメインにクールに仕上げた。

Notice of movie event for Oceans 13
set in a casino

Oceans 13, the crime and action movie set in a Las Vegas casino. The alphabet was mainly used to convey all aspects of the gorgeous environment associated with a Las Vegas casino and to create a cool look.

映画輸入販売、配給 / イベントの告知
Movie Import, Sale and Distribution / Event Announcement
CL：ワーナーエンターテインメントジャパン WARNER ENTERTAINMENT JAPAN
CD：浅尾浩一 Koichi Asao   AD：青井達也 Tatsuya Aoi
D：山崎弘幸 Hiroyuki Yamazaki
DF, SB：ノーザングラフィックス Northern Graphics

メロディのプレゼントも添えられた
クリスマスカード

表紙の丸い窓から雪の結晶をのぞかせクリスマスムードを演出。表紙のブラックとは対照的に中面はホワイトクリスマスを連想させる白が基調となっている。QRコードがついており、アクセスすると音楽が聴けるというちょっとしたプレゼントもついている。

A Christmas card that arrives together with the gift of a melody

A Christmas mood was created with snow crystals peeping out from the round window on the cover. In contrast to the black of the cover, the inside is a basic tone of white that we associate with a white Christmas. A QR code is included for accessing the music that is the Christmas present.

音楽レーベル / 季節の挨拶状
Music Label / Seasonal Greetings
CL：エースケッチ A-Sketch　AD：相澤幸彦 Yukihiko Aizawa
D：永田千奈 China Nagata　DF, SB：相澤事務所 aizawa office

楽しい時間を予感させる
ジャズライブの告知 DM

毎年、こどもの日に開催される大人のためのジャズライブ『STAGE 505』。数字の『0』の中に、子供のような大人たちの楽しいひとときを表現した。

DM giving notice of a live jazz event containing hints of a fun time

The Stage 505 live jazz event for grown-ups held every year on Children's Day. The same kind of fun time that children have was expressed inside the numeral 0.

ジャズライブ / イベントの告知
Jazz Live / Event Announcement
CL：ステージ505 STAGE505
CD：直野秀治郎 Hidejiro Naono
AD, D：長澤昌彦 Masahiko Nagasawa
DF, SB：マヒコ Mahiko

人が曲線に恋することはあるのか。

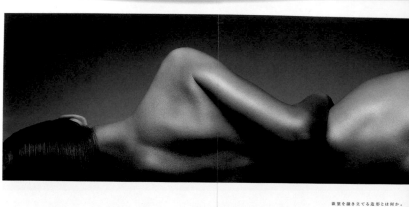

欲望を掻き立てる造形とは何か。

New Audi A5 Debut

商品の魅力であるボディラインに
クローズアップした展示会招待状

ボディラインが特徴であるAudi A5。この魅力を表現するためモノクロ調の写真をメインに用い、美しい女性のボディラインとプロダクトを対比させた。シンプルながら洗練されたデザインにより、より商品の特徴を引き立てる仕上がりとなった。

Exhibition invitation featuring a close-up of the most captivating part of the product, the bodyline

The Audi A5 with its characteristic bodyline. To express the attractiveness of the bodyline, a black-and-white style photograph was used a key visual and compared to the bodyline of a beautiful woman. Although simple, the sophisticated design enhances the characteristics of the product.

自動車輸入・販売 / 展示会の招待状
Motor Vehicle Import and Sale /
New Model Debut Event Invitation
CL：アウディジャパン　Audi Japan K.K.
CD：Mark Collis　AD：中川 勉　Tsutomu Nakagawa
D：辻岡優作　Yusaku Tsujioka　P：田島一成　Kazunari Tajima
SB：オグルヴィ・アンド・メイザー・ジャパン　Ogilvy & Mather Japan

ボタンを押すとエンジン音が鳴る、
体感型展示会招待状

パワフルなエンジンを搭載したニューモデルのデビューを、
既存モデル購入者に訴求するため、ボタンを押すとエンジン
音が鳴るギミックを施した。ニューモデルのデザインや機能
性だけでなく、その特徴を実際に体感できることでインパク
トをあたえた。

An interactive invitation to an exhibition which when the button is pressed, emits the roar of an engine.

As a way of marketing the new model Audi equipped with
a powerful engine to existing owners of the current model,
a gimmick was devised where the sound of the engine was
heard when the button was pressed. The gimmick added
impact by providing an experience not only of the design and
functionality of the new model but its special characteristics
also.

自動車輸入・販売 / 展示会の招待状
Motor Vehicle Import and Sale /
New Model Debut Event Invitation
CL：アウディジャパン　Audi Japan K.K.
CD：Mark Collis　AD：中川 勉　Tsutomu Nakagawa
D：脇本 忍　Shinobu Wakimoto (Tribune)
SB：オグルヴィ・アンド・メイザー・ジャパン　Ogilvy & Mather Japan

ワインのコルクを抜くときの楽しみ

コルクを外すと中身が読める、ワインボトルの形をしたDM。

The joy of popping the cork on a bottle of wine

A DM in the shape of a wine bottle where the contents can be read when the cork is removed.

広告 / イベント告知
Advertising / Event Announcement
CL：HAKUHODO Records
D, SB：中臺隆平　Ryuhei Nakadai

趣向をこらしたイベントプロデュース会社の年賀状

2009年の丑年にちなみ、牛肉に見立てたカードをパック加工した年賀状を作成。パックの上にはラベルを貼り原産地名に社名、原材料名に社員の名前を記載という遊び心を盛り込んだ楽しい年賀状となった。

An elaborate New Year's card for an event production company

In 2009, the Year of the Ox, the card was put through a packing process to resemble beef. The result was a New Year's card that was fun and funny where a label was applied to the top of the pack and the employees' names were listed under raw ingredients.

イベントプロデュース / 季節の挨拶状
Event Produce / Seasonal Greetings
CL：ツミキプロモーション　tsumiki promotion　AD, D：青井達也　Tatsuya Aoi
DF, SB：ノーザングラフィックス　Northern Graphics

アイデアの探求を金塊探しで表現、ONE SHOW 2008 展案内状

『アイデアを生むことは金塊を掘り起こすようなもの』をコンセプトに、アイデアを探求するクリエイターの努力や労力、ひらめきを黒と白とゴールドでシニカルに展開。ざらついた紙で地中を掘っているような手触りを伝えた。封筒にジッパー加工を施し、開けてゆくと自分で穴を掘ってるような感覚になれるよう仕上げた。

Equating the search for ideas with unearthing something buried in the ground for notice of the ONE SHOW 2008 exhibition

Based on the concept of "producing an idea is akin to unearthing a nugget of gold," the idea of creators searching for ideas is developed in black, white and gold. A grainy paper conveys the idea of digging underground. The envelope has a zipper opening to enhance the idea of digging a hole.

財団法人 / イベントの告知   Juristic Foundation / Event Announcement
CL：吉田秀雄記念事業財団 Yoshida Hideo Memorial Foundation / アド・ミュージアム東京 ADVERTISING MUSEUM TOKYO
AD：八木義博 Yoshihiro Yagi   D：木村 洋 Yo Kimura   CW：古川裕也 Yuya Furukawa / 筒井晴子 Haruko Tsutsui
Agency：電通 DENTSU INC. / カタチ Katachi,. Co Ltd.   P：おやまめぐみ Megumi Oyama
Printing：在本 剛 Tsuyoshi Arimoto   SB：電通 DENTSU INC.

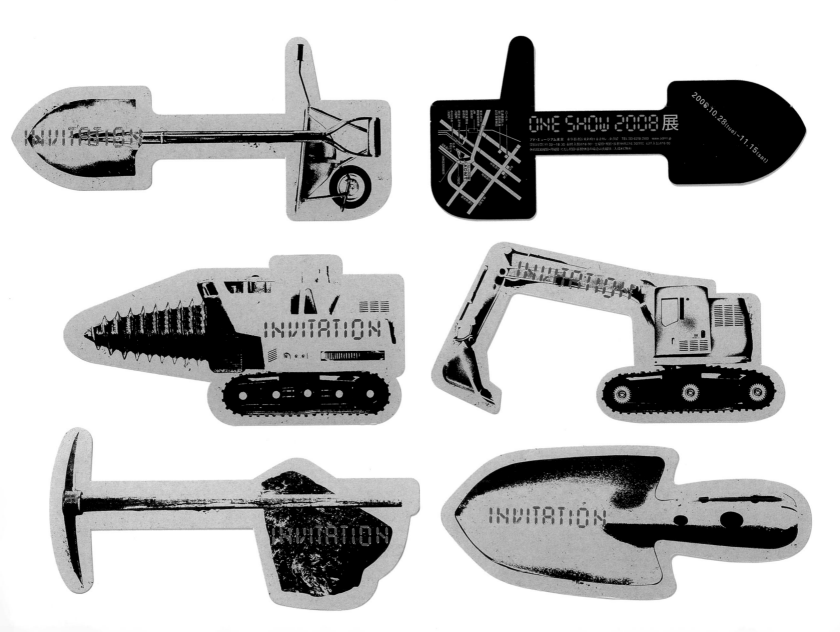

折ることでモノづくりの楽しさを表現、D&AD賞 2008展案内状

D&ADのシンボルカラーである黄色と黒をメインに2種類制作。ひとつは折ると受賞者に贈られるペンシル型トロフィーの形になり、封筒兼DMとして送付できる。もう一方は折ると六角形のロゴの形になり、DVDのパッケージとしても使用可能。ヨーロッパのポスターのような雰囲気や手触りを感じられるデザインにした。

Expressing the pleasure of making things from folded paper for notice of the D&AD 2008 exhibition

Produced in two types with the D&AD symbol colors of yellow and black. One of them when folded becomes the pencil-shaped trophy presented to award winners, which can also be sent as a combined DM and envelope. The other one when folded turns into the hexagonal logo, which can also be used as DVD packaging. The aim of the design was to create the look and texture of a European-style poster.

財団法人 / イベントの告知   Juristic Foundation / Event Announcement
CL：吉田秀雄記念事業財団 Yoshida Hideo Memorial Foundation / アド・ミュージアム東京 ADVERTISING MUSEUM TOKYO
CD：古川裕也 Yuya Furukawa   AD：八木義博 Yoshihiro Yagi   D：木村 洋 Yo Kimura   CW：筒井晴子 Haruko Tsutsui
Agency：電通 DENTSU INC. / カタチ Katachi,. Co Ltd.   P：おやまめぐみ Megumi Oyama   Printing：在本 剛 Tsuyoshi Arimoto
SB：電通 DENTSU INC.

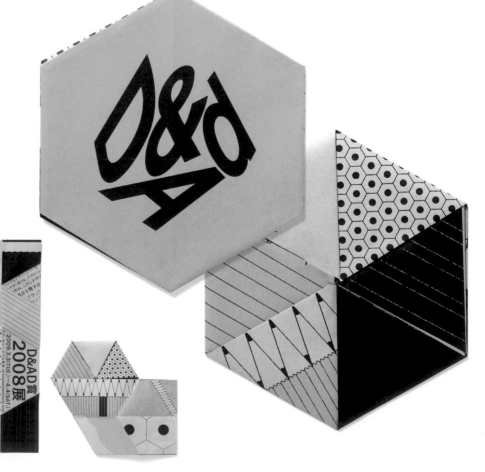

JAGDA TOKYO 第4回展覧会　秋田 寛＋長井健太郎 二人展

アルファベットで作成された漢字が印象的な企画展告知DM

用紙のホログラムによる色彩変化をビジュアルとして扱った。ロゴタイプはスミ単色UV印刷で、シンプル＆インパクトのあるデザインにした。

Exhibition announcement with kanji characters impressively created using the alphabet

Changes of color caused by holograms in the paper were treated as visuals. The logo-type was UV-printed in the single color of charcoal to create a simple design that had impact.

グラフィックデザイン企画展 / 企画展告知　Graphic Design Exhibition / Event Announcement
CL: JAGDA TOKYO 第4回展覧会 秋田 寛＋長井健太郎 二人展　JAGDA TOKYO 04 Akita Kan + Nagai Kentaro Exhibition
CD, AD：秋田 寛　Kan Akita　D：長井健太郎　Kentaro Nagai　DF：アキタ・デザイン・カン　Akita Design Kan Inc.
DF, SB：グラフレックスディレクションズ　Graflex Directions

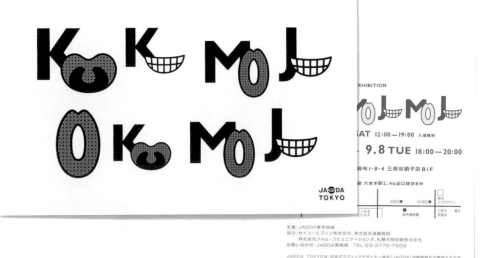

展覧会のテーマである
文字をモチーフにデザインした招待状

『JAGDA TOKYO』で開催された『柿木原政広×岡田善敬』展のオープニングパーティ招待状。文字をモチーフとした展覧会であるため、ローマ字の母音を口の形で読ませるなど、DMのデザインも文字で遊んだ。コート紙にマットブラックインキを使用し、目を引くものに。

An invitation designed with a motif of the letters that were the theme of the exhibition

An invitation to the opening of the Kakinokihara Masahiro x Okada Yoshinori Exhibition head at JAGDA Tokyo. As letters were the exhibition's motif, the DM also had fun with them, for example, the shape of a mouth sounding out English vowels. Matte black ink was used on coated paper to catch the eye.

デザインギャラリー /
展覧会の招待状、オープニングパーティの招待状
Design Gallery /
Exhibition Invitation, Opening Party Invitation
CL：ジャグダトウキョウ　JAGDA TOKYO
AD, D：岡田善敬　Yoshinori Okada
DF, SB：札幌大同印刷　SAPPORO DAIDO PRINTING Co., Ltd.

『OPEN』をキーワードに展開したイベント告知

武蔵野美術大学の2009年度オープンキャンパスのデザイン計画DM。オープンキャンパス・学校開放・日常公開という
それぞれの意味が込められた『OPEN』。来場した学生達に『目標が見えた』『新しい発見があった』など様々な『OPEN』
を感じてもらえるよう心がけた。

Developing the keyword "open" for notice of an event

A DM announcing the design plan for the 2009 Musashino Art University open campus. The word "open" contains various
meanings including open campus, open school, open to the everyday. The aim was to make the students who visited the
campus understand the various meanings of "open" (for example, "You can see your goals" and "new discoveries.")

大学 / イベントの告知   University / Event Announcement
CL：武蔵野美術大学 Musashino Art University   AD, D：古屋貴広 Takahiro Furuya   Producer：種市一寛 Kazuhiro Taneichi
DF, SB：フラットルーム FLATROOM

さまざまな『カタチ』を
コンセプトに制作した展示会の招待状

コンセプトはさまざまな『カタチ』。生徒と作品の集合をタイトルテキス
トから連動してデザインされた。白を基調にすっきりとまとめつつ、散り
ばめられたさまざまなカタチがアクセントとなっている。

A concept of various "forms" for an invitation to an exhibition

The concept was various "forms." The DM was designed for the title
text to link the students and collections of work. The design is coherently
put together with a basic tone of white and the various shapes scattered
throughout serve as accents.

大学 / 卒業制作学外展の招待状
University / Exhibition of Graduation Works Invitation
CL：女子美術大学 Joshibi University of Art and Design   D：永田千奈 China Nagata
DF, SB：相澤事務所 aizawa office

OPEN

MUSASHINO ART UNIVERSITY
OPEN CAMPUS 2009
2009.6.13(SAT)—14(SUN)

'OPEN' YOUR SENSE.   'OPEN' YOUR MIND.   'OPEN' YOUR DREAM.   'OPEN' YOUR HEART.   'OPEN' YOUR FUTURE.   'OPEN' YOUR MAU LIFE!

告知だけでなく、出席後も飾れるように作成した授賞式の招待状

優れた広告の制作者に贈られるTCC賞授賞式の招待状。トロフィーとともに飾れるよう、告知面の裏を金屏風に。コストダウンも考慮し、キュリアスメタルの紙に特色のベージュを敷くことで、落ち着いた金色を表現。『おめでとう』の文字をサラリと入れるため金箔を使用し、艶のある金箔と艶消しの金屏風で品良く仕上げた。

Invitation to an award ceremony produced not only as an invitation but also as something decorative for after the event

An invitation to the TCC award ceremony where awards are presented to outstanding advertising producers. The back of the invitation was designed to resemble a gold folding screen to be displayed alongside the trophy. To reduce costs, an understated gold color was produced by applying a special beige color to Curious Metal paper. Gold foil was used sleekly to insert the word "Congratulations" and the glossy gold leaf and the matte gold folding screen were given a refined finish.

コピーライター・CMプランナー団体 / 授賞式の招待状
Copywriters and Commercial Planners Group / Invitation to an Award
CL：東京コピーライターズクラブ　Tokyo Copywriters Club
AD, D：平井秀和　Hidekazu Hirai　CW：岩田秀紀（I&S BBDO）
Hidenori Iwata（I&S BBDO）　DF, SB：ピースグラフィックス　Peace Graphics

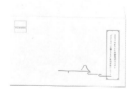

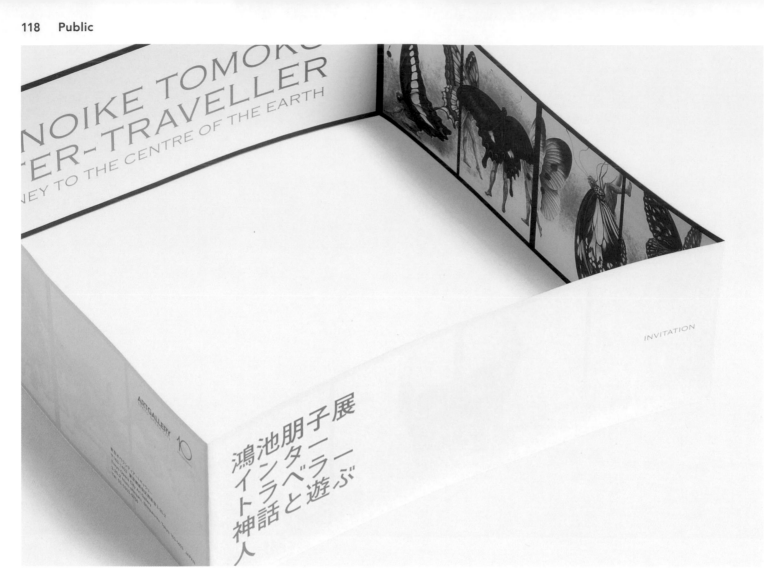

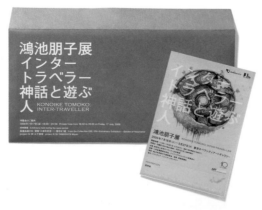

作品とタイトルの強度を拮抗させ、
展示の世界観を表現した内覧会招待状

鴻池朋子展『インタートラベラー 神話と遊ぶ人』の招待状。
新作である12面の襖絵を内面に配し、開くと作品が立ち上が
る仕組み。縮小スケールながら、作品の迫力と全体像をチラシ
と連動させ、隠された世界を垣間見るという展覧会のテーマ『地
球の中心への旅』と結びつけた。

**An invitation that pits the strength of the art
and the title against each other to express
the worldview of the exhibition**

An invitation to the opening of the Tomoko Konoike exhibition,
Inter-Traveller. Twelve fusuma paintings that are part of her
recent work have been arranged on the inside and designed
to stand up when the invitation is opened. Although they have
been reduced in scale, the force and the perspective of the
paintings have been incorporated into the leaflet and tied to the
theme of the exhibition "journey to the center of the earth" that
catches a glimpse of a secret world.

美術館（アートギャラリー）/ 内覧会の招待状
Art Museum（Art Gallery）/ Exhibition Invitation
CL：東京オペラシティ文化財団 Tokyo Opera City Cultural Foundation
AD, D：大島依提亜 Idea Oshima
DF：大島デザイン室 Oshima Idea Design
SB：東京オペラシティアートギャラリー Tokyo Opera City Art Gallery

キービジュアルと連動させたオープニングパーティの招待状

『日本が世界に誇れる手』をコンセプトに開催された『第9回 Japan Fashion Week in Tokyo』。手をキャンバスに制作されたキービジュアルとDMなどのツールを連動させ、マス広告の露出の少なさをカバーし、イベントの認知を上げイメージの醸成を狙った。

An invitation to an opening party that links to a key visual

The ninth Japan Fashion Week in Tokyo based on the concept of "The hands that make Japan proud throughout the world." The hand produced on canvas as the key visual were linked to the DM and other promotional tools. The aim was to compensate for lack of exposure in mass-media advertising, raise the level of public recognition and develop the image for the event.

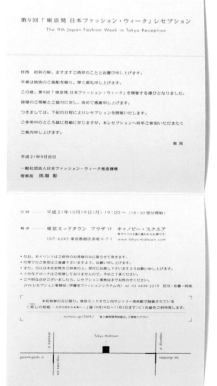

社団法人 / オープニングパーティの招待状
Corporation / Opening Party Invitation
CL：日本ファッション・ウィーク推進機構　Japan Fashion Week Organization
CD, AD, SB：中嶋貴久　Takahisa Nakajima　D：上野友和　Tomokazu Ueno
P：安彦幸枝　Sachie Abiko　I：宮島亜希　Aki Miyajima　DF：ディッシュ　dish

ブランドの歴史とスペシャル感にこだわった展覧会案内状

『ザ・ノース・フェイス』がブランド誕生40周年を記念して開催したイベント『DO MORE WITH LESS』展のレセプションパーティ招待状。DMには、アーカイブ商品やアートワークなどブランドの歴史的なシーンを掲載。封筒や文字には箔押しを使用し、スペシャル感を演出した。

Exhibition announcement emphasizing the history of the brand and a sense of specialness

A party invitation for the "Do More With Less" exhibition held by The North Face to celebrate the 40th anniversary of the brand. Historic scenes of the brand including archive products and artwork were printed in the DM. Foil was used on the envelope and the lettering to produce a sense of specialness.

スポーツ用品メーカー、複合文化施設 / 展覧会の招待状
Sporting Goods Maker, Cultural Complex / Exhibition Invitation
CL：ゴールドウイン　GOLDWIN / スパイラル / ワコールアートセンター
SPIRAL / Wacoal Art Center
AD, D, SB,：グルーヴィジョンズ　groovisions

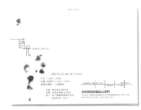

『火薬ドローイング』で
日本の春夏秋冬を描いた個展の招待状

ニューヨークを拠点に活動している中国出身の現代美術家、蔡國強（ツァイ・グォチャン）の『時光-蔡國強と資生堂』展。火薬を使用する作風であるため、あたかも紙が燃えたような、火の焦げあと感をDMにも表現。レーザー技術で細かくリアルな焦げ残りを再現し、作品の一部が送られてきたかのような錯覚を狙った。

An invitation to a solo exhibition that depicts Japan's four seasons in "gunpowder drawings"

The Light Passage-Cai Guo-Qiang & Shiseido exhibition by New York-based Chinese contemporary artist Cai Guo-Qiang. As his artistic practice often involves the use of gunpowder, the idea of the ashes left after burning paper was used in the DM also. Laser technology was used to reproduce real burn marks to create the illusion that a part of his work had been enclosed with the invitation.

化粧品メーカー / 展覧会の招待状　Cosmetics Maker / Exhibition Invitation
CL：資生堂　Shiseido Company, Limited　AD, D：青木康子　Yasuko Aoki
SB：パンゲア　PANGAEA Ltd.

北欧の日用品の普遍的な美や温かみが自然に感じられる内覧会招待状

『北欧モダン デザイン＆クラフト』展の招待状。身近な日用品を長く大切に使う北欧生活の『身の回り』の感覚が感じられるような案内状は北欧のテキスタイル（テーブルクロス）をイメージし、チケットはコースター仕様に。日用品を展示物としてではなく、室内の中に配置して撮り下ろしたメインビジュアルが、用の美や温かみを自然に伝えている。

An invitation that conveys the universal beauty and warmth of daily life products from Scandinavia in a natural way

An invitation to the Nordic Modernism: Design & Crafts exhibition. So as to convey a sense of the familiar daily life products that have long been a valued part of Scandinavian life, the exhibition announcement featured an image of a Scandinavian textile (a tablecloth), and tickets were produced as coasters. To convey the beauty and warmth of functionality in a natural way, a main visual was taken with the exhibition items arranged around an actual room.

美術館（アートギャラリー）/ 内覧会の招待状
Art Museum（Art Gallery）/ Exhibition Invitation
CL：東京オペラシティ文化財団　Tokyo Opera City Cultural Foundation
AD, D：大島依提亜　Idea Oshima
DF：大島デザイン室　Ohima Idea Design
P（Flyer）：高橋ヨーコ　Yoko Takahashi
Styling（Flyer）：岡尾美代子　Miyoko Ōkao
SB：東京オペラシティアートギャラリー　Tokyo Opera City Art Gallery

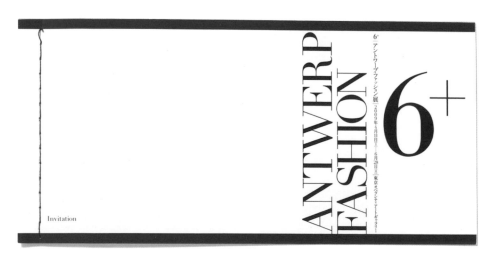

アートギャラリー初のファッション展に向けた内覧会招待状

『6＋ アントワープ・ファッション展』の招待状。アントワープ市のカラーを採用し、2色刷りという抑えた選択肢ながら、ファッションの華やかさと歴史性を感じさせる仕上がりに。6人のデザイナーを中心に、カメラマンやメイクアップなどファッションを支えるクリエイターを『＋』として表し、『6＋』のロゴを印象的に配置。

An invitation to a party for the first fashion exhibition at an art gallery

An invitation to the 6+ Antwerp Fashion Exhibition. Using the colors of the city of Antwerp and exercising the option of two-color printing, the design conveys fashion's gaiety and sense of history. Led by six designers, the creative people who support fashion such as the photographer and makeup artists were indicated with a + and the 6+ logo positioned for maximum effect.

美術館（アートギャラリー）/ 内覧会の招待状
Art Museum（Art Gallery）/ Exhibition Invitation
CL：東京オペラシティ文化財団　Tokyo Opera City Cultural Foundation
AD, D：森 大志郎　Daishiro Mori
SB：東京オペラシティアートギャラリー　Tokyo Opera City Art Gallery

『見る人に何かを期待させるデザイン』を目指した招待状

JETRO は日本のアパレル製品の認知度向上のため、パリで開催される『ATMOSPHÈRE'S展』に参加。DMは、パリの展示会でデザイナーが一堂に集まり、技・センスを披露するイメージと、楽しい演目が続くサーカスのワクワク感を重ねたデザインに。女性らしさ、華々しさの象徴としてスパンコールの写真を使用した。

An invitation aiming to create a sense of anticipation in the viewer

JETRO participated in the ATMOSPHÈRE'S exhibition held in Paris that is designed to raise the recognition level for Japanese apparel products. The DM was designed with an image of the skill and style displayed by the designers gathered together in the Paris exhibition venue and the circus-like sense of excitement as the fun program of events progressed. Photographs of spangles were used as symbols of femininity and brilliance.

独立行政法人 / 展示会の招待状
Government-related Organization / Fashion Show Invitation
CL：日本貿易振興機構 JETRO　DF, SB：セルディビジョン CELL DIVISION

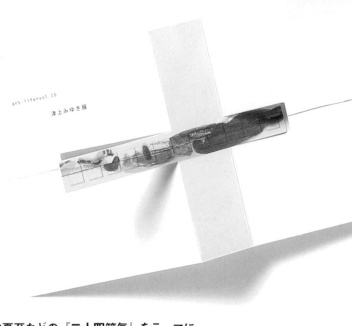

春分や夏至などの『二十四節気』をテーマに
描いた個展の招待状

津上みゆき展『24 seasons』の招待状。二十四節気という暦をモチーフにした、切れ目のないテーマの作品のため、DMも表裏の区切りのないイメージで作成。折りと型抜きを採用し、折りの伸び縮みを利用して型抜き部分が回転する仕掛けに。回転時に起こる小さな風や動きで、脈々と続く時間や空間、自然を表現した。

An invitation to a solo exhibition with the theme of "the 24 seasons of the old calendar" including the spring equinox and summer solstice

An invitation to the "24 seasons" exhibition by Miyuki Tsugami. As her work has a motif of the 24 seasons of the old calendar and a theme without end, the DM also was produced without a juncture between the front and the back. The elasticity of the folds in the DM was used to rotate the die-cut sections. The slight movement of air that occurs when the cut-out is rotated expresses time, space and nature that continues ceaselessly.

文化施設運営 / 展覧会の招待状
Cultural Facility Operation / Exhibition Invitation
CL：ワコールアートセンター Wacoal Art Center Co., Ltd.   AD, D：青木康子 Yasuko Aoki
SB：パンゲア PANGAEA Ltd.

オープニング・トークのご案内 ＜要予約＞
2007.8.28 tue. 17:00-18:30

料金別納郵便

African American Quilts:
Women Piecing Memories and Dreams
アフリカン・アメリカン・キルト─ 記憶と希望をつなぐ女性たち

糸をポイントにしてキルトの温かみを表現した
企画展の招待状

『アフリカン・アメリカン・キルト─記憶と希望をつなぐ女性たち』展の招待状。アフリカ系アメリカ人の女性たちの手作業によるキルト作品であるため、封筒に本物の糸を縫い付けるなど、糸をテーマにして手作りの温かみを表現。カタログまで一貫したイメージを踏襲できる構成にした。

An invitation to an exhibition that expresses the warmth of hand-made quilts based on the theme of thread

An invitation to the African American Quilts: Women Piecing Memories and Dreams exhibition. As the quilts were produced manually by African-American women, the warmth of hand-made objects was expressed with the theme of thread and real thread was sewn onto the envelope. The invitation was structured to achieve a consistent image throughout, including the catalogue.

化粧品メーカー / 展覧会の招待状   Cosmetics Maker / Exhibition Invitation
CL：資生堂 Shiseido Company, Limited   AD, D：青木康子 Yasuko Aoki
SB：パンゲア PANGAEA Ltd.

桐の箱に近い紙を使用して制作した
展覧会の案内

本来、保存具として創られた箱や袋もそれ自体が鑑賞の対象となり、陶器に付加価値を与える役割を持つようになったという展覧会のテーマを、お宝（焼き物）を入れる桐の箱をメインビジュアルにして表現。小・中学生向けのガイドであるため、より興味を持ってもらえるよう箱を立体的に見せた。

Information on an exhibition using paper similar to a paulownia box

The theme of the exhibition that, essentially, the boxes and bags created for storing the ceramics have themselves become objects of appreciation and that they serve to give added value to ceramics was expressed with the key visual of a paulownia box for storing valuables (ceramics). With the exhibition guide for primary and secondary students, the box was shown as three-dimensional to increase the level of interest.

公立美術館 / 企画展案内、小中学生向けの展示ガイド
National Art Museum /
Exhibition Guide for Primary and Secondary Students
CL：茨城県陶芸美術館 Ibaraki ceramic art museum
CD：花井久穂（茨城県陶芸美術館）Hisaho Hanai (Ibaraki ceramic art museum)
AD, D：笹目亮太郎 Ryotaro Sasame
P（Box）：尾見重治 Shigeharu Omi   DF, SB：スプラウト Sprout

トレペを使い作品の写真を活かした
オープニング・レセプションの招待状

荒木経惟氏が、現代の広島に暮らす人たち461組の『顔』を撮り下ろした展覧会『荒木経惟 広島ノ顔』のオープニング・レセプション招待状。封筒のロゴが透けて重なることで、案内状の表紙の写真がより活かせるようにデザイン。また、トレペの封筒からはわからない案内状の用紙のキラキラ感で、開封したときの驚きを演出した。

An invitation to an opening that maximizes the photographic artwork using tracing paper

An invitation to the opening of the Nobuyoshi Araki: The Faces of Hiroshima exhibition where Nobuyoshi Araki took photographs of 450 sets of people who live in modern-day Hiroshima. Printing a transparent logo on the envelope meant that the design was better able to maximize the effect of the photographs on the cover. The sparkling paper used for the DM that could not be seen through the tracing paper envelope created a special surprise when the envelope was opened.

美術館 / オープニング・レセプションの招待状
Art Museum / Opening Reception Invitation
CL：広島市現代美術館
Hiroshima City Museum of Contemporary Art
AD, D：野村勝久 Katsuhisa Nomura   CW：大賀郁子 Ikuko Oga
DF, SB：野村デザイン制作室 NOMURA DESIGN FACTORY

アーティストとアートファンが集う日本発アートフェアの告知DM

世界中のアーティストが出展する、日本発のアートの祭典『GEISAI#12』の告知＆招待状。アーティストとアートファンのコミュニケーションの場であることから、POPなデザインと色遣いで楽しさや親しみやすさを表現。DMにはミシン目を入れ、2名分のチケットとした。

DM announcing a Japanese art fair, a get-together of artists and art fans

Announcement and invitation to the GEISAI#12 festival featuring artwork by artists from around the world. As the festival is a forum for communication between artists and art fans, a sense of friendliness was expressed using a pop design and color scheme. Perforations were made in the DM to create tickets for two people.

アート関連事業 / イベントの告知
Art-related Business / Event Announcement
CL：GEISAI実行委員会 GEISAI Executive Committee /
カイカイキキ Kaikai Kiki Co., Ltd.
AD, D, SB：グルーヴィジョンズ groovisions

柔らかさと楽しさを伝える
ワークショップの告知カード

石見美術館がフェルト作家の濱野由美さんを招き、クリスマスの時期に開催したワークショップ『羊毛で靴下をつくろう』の告知カード。靴下の形で表面と裏面の関連性を表現し、フェルトの手触り感を出すために、ざっくりした用紙を使用。フェルトの柔らかいイメージとクリスマスの楽しいイメージを重ねた。

Workshop announcement that
conveys softness and fun

Information on the "Let's make socks with wool" workshop held in the Christmas season to which Iwami Art Museum invited the felt artist, Yumi Hamano. The relationship between the front and the back were expressed with the shape of a sock, and a rough paper was used to convey the texture of the felt. The soft image of socks and the fun image of Christmas were successfully combined.

美術館 / イベントの告知
Art Museum / Event Announcement
CL：島根県立石見美術館 IWAMI ART MUSEUM
AD, D：野村勝久 Katsuhisa Nomura
Art：濱野由美 Yumi Hamano
DF, SB：野村デザイン制作室 NOMURA DESIGN FACTORY

ファブリス・イベール『たねを育てる』展のDM兼配布用チラシ

『一枚の紙が花器へと変化する』をデザインコンセプトとし、同展に誘導するだけでなく、参加できるチラシであることを目的とした。テーマである『たねを育てる』という行為への参加でより魅力を伝えられるのではないかと考え、配布チラシを折ると鉢植えになるデザインを提案。配布時には、手作業で本物の植物の種をチラシの裏面に貼り付けた。また、鉢植えとして完成した状態でも情報が伝わるよう、ロゴの置き場所も工夫した。

Combined DM and leaflet for the Fabrice Hyber exhibition Je s'aine
With the idea of not merely attracting visitors to the exhibition but also to convey the charm of participating in the act of growing things from seeds that is the theme of the exhibition, a design where the leaflet when folded became a pot plant was suggested. When the leaflet was distributed, the seeds for a real plant were stuck manually to the back. A position for the logo was also devised so that the information was conveyed in a complete state as a pot plant.

美術館 / 展覧会の告知   Art Museum / Exhibition Announcement
CL：ワタリウム美術館 WATARI-UM AD：丹下紘希 Kouki Tange
D：浦上悠平 Yuhei Urakami DF, SB：マバタキ製作所 Mabataki Factory Inc.

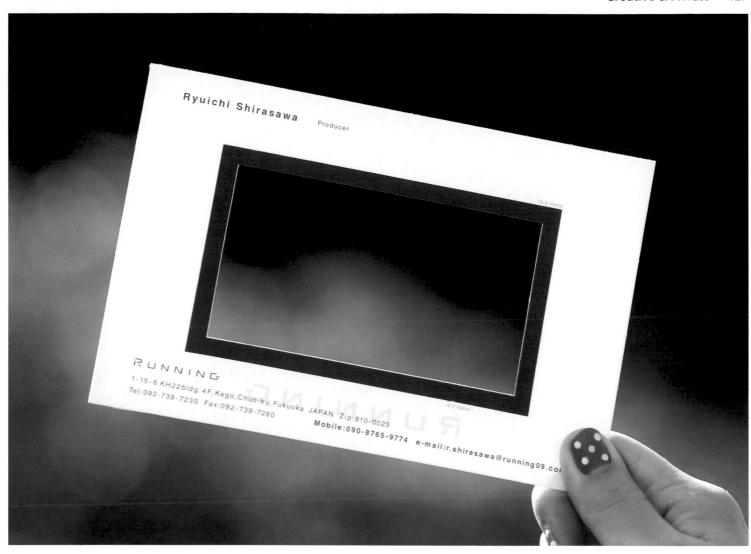

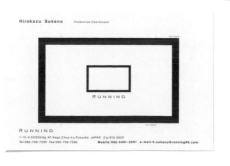

取り外して『名刺』と『フレーム』として使用できる挨拶状

ランニング社のロゴであるTVフレームをモチーフに制作。センター部分を取り外せばそのまま名刺に。また外した本体は16：9比率のフレーム枠になり、映像制作におけるフリーミングに活用可能。『フレーム越しに発見したものをいい映像、いいCMに仕上げたければ弊社まで』というメッセージも込められている。

A removable greeting card that can be used as a business card and frame
Produced with the motif of the frame of a TV, which is the Running logo. Remove the central section and you have a business card. The remaining piece turns into a 16:9 ratio frame that can be used for filming in audiovisual productions. The design also contains the message "Contact us for great images and great commercials about things you have discovered beyond the frame."

TVCM制作 / 会社設立の案内状
TV Commercial Production / Office Opening Announcement
CL：ランニング RUNNING INC.   CD, AD, D：鍵矢康紀 Yasunori Kagiya
SB：電通西日本 広島支社 DENTSU WEST JAPAN INC. HIROSHIMA

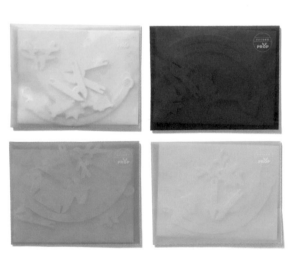

クリスマスの贈り物をイメージさせる挨拶状

クリスマスと新年に向けた会社のグリーティングカード。パッケージを工夫し、クリスマスプレゼントが届くようなワクワクした気分を演出。カード自体もデスクに飾れる立体的な構成にし、自分で組み立てたり、シールを貼ったりといった遊び心を加えた。

A greeting card with an image of a Christmas gift

A company greeting card for Christmas and the New Year. The packaging was designed to create the excitement of receiving a Christmas present. The card itself has a three-dimensional structure for displaying on a desk with the added fun of assembling it and covering it with stickers.

デザイン事務所 / 季節の挨拶状   Design Firm / Seasonal Greetings
CL, DF, SB：プロップ グラフィック ステーション PROP GRAPHIC STATION INC.   AD：南部直美 Naomi Nanbu   D：和田佳子 Yoshiko Wada

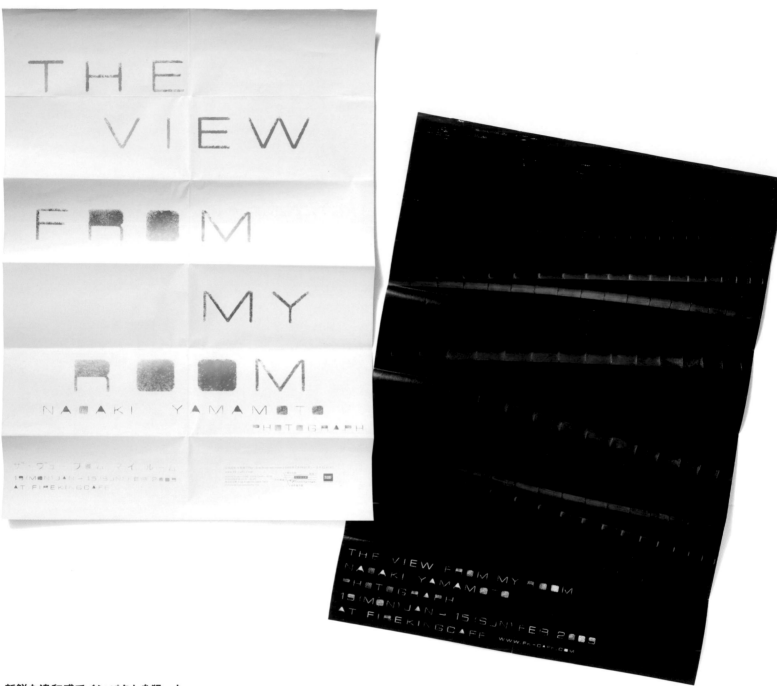

新鮮な違和感でインパクトを狙った
写真展の案内状

写真家・山本尚明の個展『THE VIEW FROM MY ROOM』のDM
兼ポスター。インパクトのある竹藪の写真のオリジナルプリントを
そのまま大判サイズのDMに。折りたたんだ状態で表1にタイトル、
表4に会場への地図がくるようレイアウトし、タイポグラフィには
ステンシルを用いた。

Creating fresh impact with a fresh sense of
incongruity for photo-exhibition announcement

A poster and DM for the solo exhibition The View From My Room by
photographer Naoaki Yamamoto. The DM shows an original print in
B0 size of a powerful photograph of a bamboo grove. When the DM
is folded, the title falls on the outside front panel and a map to the
exhibition venue on the outside back panel. Stencils were used for
the typography.

写真家 / 個展の案内状
Photographer / Exhibition Announcement

CL, P：山本尚明 Naoaki Yamamoto   CD, AD, D：関 宙明 Hiroaki Seki
DF, SB：ミスター・ユニバース mr.universe

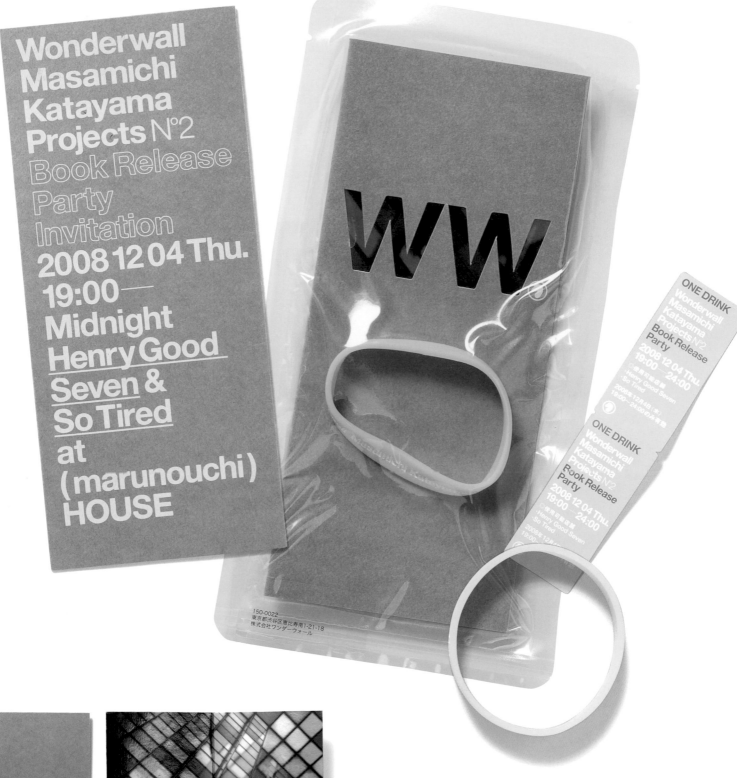

パーティーの楽しさを期待させるリストバンド付き招待状

東京で開催された片山正通氏の出版記念パーティー招待状。映像の上映やライブなども催される華やかなパーティーであるため、内面は会場の雰囲気をイメージさせるデザインに。当日の入場チケットとなるリストバンドとドリンクチケットを同封した。

An invitation with wristband attached to increase anticipation of the fun of the party

Invitation to a party held in Tokyo to celebrate the publication of Masamichi Katayama. As the gorgeous party also featured audiovisual displays and live performances, the inside of the invitation was designed to recreate the atmosphere of the party venue. Enclosed was a wristband that would become an admission ticket to the party and a drink coupon.

インテリアデザイン事務所 / 出版記念パーティの招待状
Interior Design Office / Party Invitation to Celebrate Publication

CL：ワンダーウォール Wonderwall Inc.　AD, D, SB：グルーヴィジョンズ groovisions

エキシビションを楽しむための
3D メガネ付き DM

3D グラフィックを展示した『KHA 3D EXHIBITION』の
招待状。DM に 3D メガネが付いており、DM 自体がエキ
シビションを楽しむためのツールになっている。

A DM complete with 3D glasses to have
fun with at the exhibition

An invitation to the 3D graphics KHA 3D Exhibition. 3D
glasses were attached to the DM, turning the DM itself into
a fun tool for enjoying the exhibition.

デザイン事務所 / 展示会の招待状
Design Firm / Exhibition Invitation
CL, SB：カワムラヒデオアクティビィティ Kawamura Hideo Activity Inc.
AD, D：カワムラヒデオ Hideo Kawamura

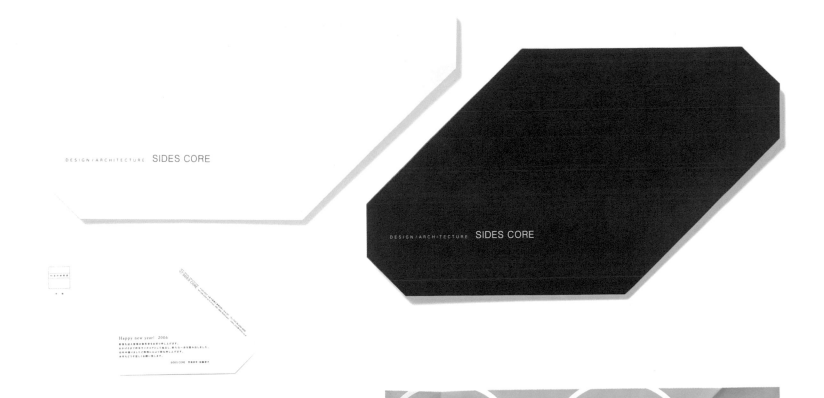

建築デザイン設計事務所の活動や展開をカタチにした年賀状

建築・インテリアのデザイン事務所『SIDES CORE』の年賀状。2006年は、その多面性を表現。通常使えるポストカードも作成した。2008年は驚きの年にしたかったため、手紙折りのような変わった折りを工夫。

New Year's cards that incorporate the activity and development of the architectural design office

New Year's cards for Sides Core who are involved in various business activities. The 2006 card expressed the multiple aspects of the company. A usable postcard was also produced. For an element of surprise in 2008, an unusual way of folding the card that resembled that of a letter was devised.

建築・インテリアのデザイン事務所 / 季節の挨拶状
Architectural Design Office / Seasonal Greetings
CL：サイズコア　SIDES CORE　CD, AD, D：古川智基　Tomoki Furukawa
DF, SB：サファリ　SAFARI inc.

a

b

c

広告制作を手がける同社のバラエティ豊かな挨拶状

移転案内（a）では『新たな場所で再スタートをきる』という想いからチェッカーフラッグのデザインで制作し、2008 年の年賀状（b）は DIC のカラーガイドをモチーフに、色はもちろん DIC2008 番を使用。2009 年（c）はクラフト紙に箔押しを施し親しみやすさと安定感を演出した。

A variety-filled greeting card for an advertising production company

The design of the change of premises notice (a) incorporated a checkered flag to express the idea of "Restart from a new spot." The one for 2008 (b) has a motif of the DIC color guide and therefore the color used is DIC2008. Kraft paper and silver foil were used for the 2009 card (c) to create a sense of familiarity and stability.

広告制作／季節の挨拶状、移転案内
Advertising Production / Seasonal Greetings, Moving Announcement
CL, DF, SB：フラットルーム FLATROOM　AD, D：中村洋太 Yota Nakamura　Producer：種市一寛 Kazuhiro Taneichi

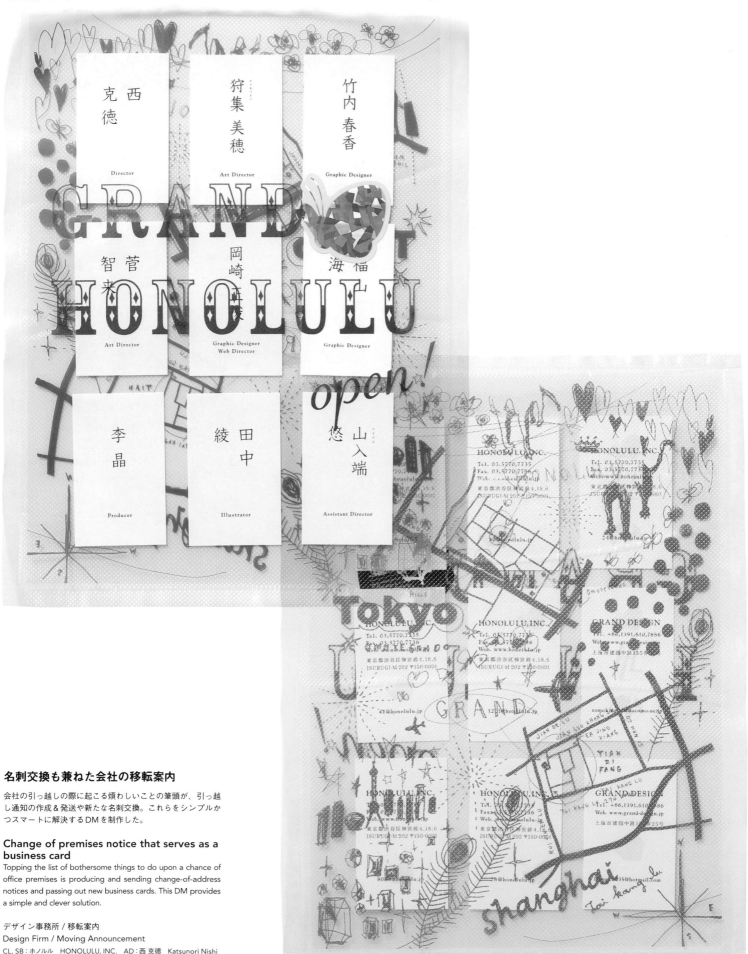

名刺交換も兼ねた会社の移転案内

会社の引っ越しの際に起こる煩わしいことの筆頭が、引っ越し通知の作成＆発送や新たな名刺交換。これらをシンプルかつスマートに解決するDMを制作した。

Change of premises notice that serves as a business card

Topping the list of bothersome things to do upon a chance of office premises is producing and sending change-of-address notices and passing out new business cards. This DM provides a simple and clever solution.

デザイン事務所 / 移転案内
Design Firm / Moving Announcement
CL, SB：ホノルル　HONOLULU, INC.　AD：西 克徳　Katsunori Nishi
D：田中 綾　Aya Tanaka

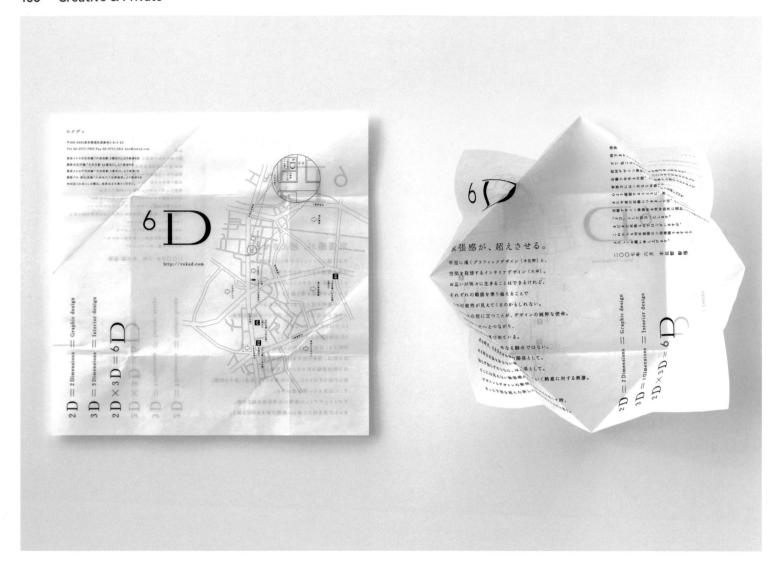

折りを効果的に使用した会社設立案内

1枚の紙に挨拶文、会社の地図、ロゴ、全ての要素が入っている案内状。
正方形に折り畳み、宛名のステッカーで封をして郵送するため、封筒
を使用せずに成立する機能的なデザインとなっている。

An effective use of folds for information on establishment of a company

Information that on one sheet of paper contains greetings, a map of
the company, a logo and all the elements. Folded up into a square, it
was sealed with the address sticker and sent in the post, meaning a
functional design that did not require the use of envelopes.

デザイン事務所 /設立案内
Design Firm / Office Opening Announcement
CL, DF, SB：ロクディ　6D　AD, D：木住野彰悟　Shogo Kishino
P：藤本伸吾 Shingo Fujimoto (hue)

株式会社設立のお知らせ

盛夏の候、時下ますますご清祥の段、お慶び申し上げますとともに、
平素より格別のご厚誼にあずかり、厚く御礼申し上げます。
お陰様で room-composite は、2007年7月3日付けで法人格を取得しました。
今後とも、より柔軟で質の高いクリエイティブを、皆様に提供差し上げることに尽力いたします。
尚一層のご指導、ご鞭撻を賜りますよう、よろしくお願い申し上げます。

※経理・経営上の運営に置きましては法人商号を使用させていただきますが、
制作進行上での呼称は引き続き「room-composite」「カイシトモヤ」とさせていただきます。

法人商号　　株式会社 ルームコンポジット　　room-composite co., ltd.
代表取締役　　海士智也

http://www.room-composite.com
kaishi@room-composite.com
090-7250-9362 (mobile phone)　　03-3481-4562 (TEL with FAX)
〒155-0031 東京都世田谷区北沢3-24-14 サニーコート1-A

用紙：竹尾「波光」200kg(四六)+村田金箔スタンダードメタリックホイル・つや消し金 No.102+DIC2271
Printed by Soundgraphics Inc. ©2007 room-composite co., ltd.

デコラティブな構成でインパクトを狙った会社法人化の案内

『法人化』の『法』の漢字をデコラティブなパターンで構成し、インパクトのある表現を狙った。『法』の文字は金箔押しを施している。

Announcement of the incorporation of a company, the aim being to create impact with decorative construction

To create impact, the first kanji character in the word "incorporation" was created in a decorative pattern. The same character was then covered in gold foil.

デザイン事務所 / 法人化の案内
Design Firm /
Company Incorporation Announcement
CL, SB：ルームコンポジット　room-composite
AD, D：カイシトモヤ　Tomoya Kaishi

ゴールドとエンボスを使用して ゴージャス感を出した年賀状

2009年が丑年であるため、『Cow Parade Tokyo』（実物大のグラスファイバー製の牛にペイントして街中に展示するイベント）で制作した牛のオブジェを起用。ゴールド、エンボス加工を施し、ゴージャス感を演出した。

A gorgeous New Year's card with gold and embossing

As 2009 was the Year of the Ox, a cow objet produced for the Cow Parade Tokyo (the event where a life-size fibre-glass cow was painted and displayed on the street) was used. Touches of gorgeousness were added with gold and an embossing process.

デザイン事務所 / 季節の挨拶状
Design Firm / Seasonal Greetings
CL, SB：カワムラヒデオアクティビィティ
Kawamura Hideo Activity Inc.
AD, D：カワムラヒデオ　Hideo Kawamura

立体的な構造で開けたときのインパクトを狙った移転案内

ルーフガーデンのある事務所に移転したため、箱庭をモチーフにした移転案内を作成。送付時は平らな状態だが、受け取った人が開けてはじめて立体的な箱になるよう構造を工夫。底の芝の部分には柔らかいグラスシートを敷き、その上に案内状を載せた。開口部にはミシン目を入れ、お菓子を開けるようなワクワク感を喚起。

Change of premises notice that creates impact when unfolded with a three-dimensional structure

As the company had moved to an office with a roof garden, the change of premises notice was produced with a motif of a box garden. The notice is in a two-dimensional form when sent, but designed to become a three-dimensional box when unfolded by the recipient. Soft glass sheets were laid on the turf section at the bottom and the notice placed on top. The opening was perforated to create the same feeling of excitement as when opening a box of candy.

WEB制作会社 / 移転案内   Web Production / Moving Announcement
CL：ゾーンプログラム zoneprogram inc.   AD, D, P：平井秀和 Hidekazu Hirai   DF, SB：ピースグラフィックス Peace Graphics

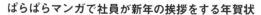

ぱらぱらマンガで社員が新年の挨拶をする年賀状

社員が増え、顔見せの挨拶をしたいという意向から誕生した年賀状。顔写真を並べるだけでは一度見ただけで終わってしまうが、ぱらぱらマンガ（フリップブック）にすることで、繰り返し見てもらえるものに。めくると社員が「ハッピーニューイヤー」と言っている。あえて中身が見えるように、透明な真空パックで送付した。

A New Year's card where employees send greetings via a flipbook

A New Year's card originating in the idea that new employees wished formally to introduce themselves to the rest of the company. The idea could have been confined to merely arranging rows of photographs of the faces of new employees so that everyone would be seen at one time, but presenting the idea in the form of a flipbook meant that the card would be looked at more than once. The card was inserted into a vacuum-pack bag so that the contents were visible from the outside.

WEB制作会社 / 季節の挨拶状
Web Production / Seasonal Greetings
CL：ゾーンプログラム zoneprogram inc.
AD, D, P：平井秀和 Hidekazu Hirai
DF, SB：ピースグラフィックス Peace Graphics

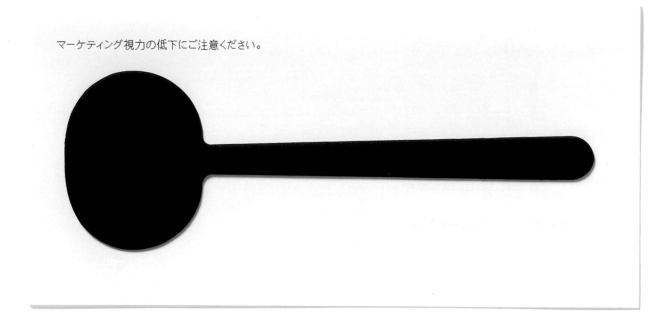

マーケティング視力の低下にご注意ください。

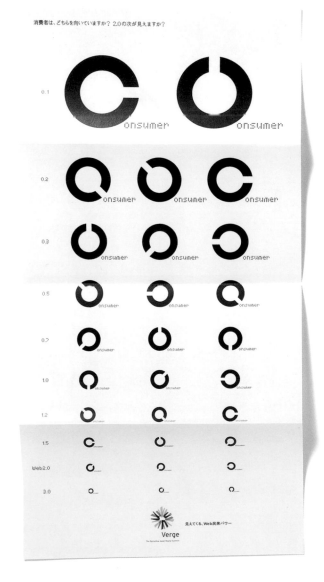

視力検診で問いかけと再認識の効果を狙った
セミナー告知DM

同社主催のパートナー向けセミナー告知DM。セミナーのサブタイトルは『見えてくる、Web民衆パワー』。DMでは『消費者はどちらを向いていますか？ 2.0の次が見えますか？』というキャッチコピーで視力検査をモチーフに制作。開封率を高めるため透明封筒を使用し、検査時に必要な片目を隠す器具も同封した。

DM notice of a seminar drawing on the effects of asking questions and renewed appreciation in an eye examination
A DM notice of a seminar hosted by the company for its partners, subtitled "Web people power coming soon." The DM contains the catch copy "Which way are consumers facing? Can you see what comes after 2.0?" and a motif of an eye-exam chart. A transparent envelope was used to reduce the discard-without-opening rate and contains the tool used to cover one of the eyes in an eye examination.

広告代理店 / イベントの告知   Advertising Agency / Event Announcement
CL, SB：オグルヴィ・ワン・ジャパン OgilvyOne Japan   CD：三好尊信 Takanobu Miyoshi
AD：橋本孝久 Takahisa Hashimoto   D：徳丸達也 Tatsuya Tokumaru
CW：澤田修治 Syuji Sawada

工夫と仕掛けを盛りこんだサービス案内DM

同社業務の『展示会出展サポート』の営業ツールとして制作したDM。多忙なビジネスマンに『任せて楽してください』というメッセージを込め『らくちん』な雰囲気でまんがを軸に構成。中面の飛び出す切り絵は手作業で張り込み、名刺収納ケースも装着。同社のサービス精神を感じてもらえるよう工夫と仕掛けを盛り込んだ。

DM packed with devices and mechanisms announcing services

A DM produced as a sales tool for the company's exhibition support service. The message is "Relax and leave it to us" and the DM has been structured around a relaxed-style manga. The pop-up illustrations have been applied manually and a business card storage case is attached. The company's spirit of service has been incorporated into the design using various devices.

広告代理店 / サービス案内　Advertising Agency / Service Information

CL, DF, SB：アドアージュ　Adage Corporation　CD：掛谷幸恵　Yukie Kakeya　AD, D：手嶋民夫　Tamio Teshima
I, Cartoon：工藤志帆　Shiho Kudo

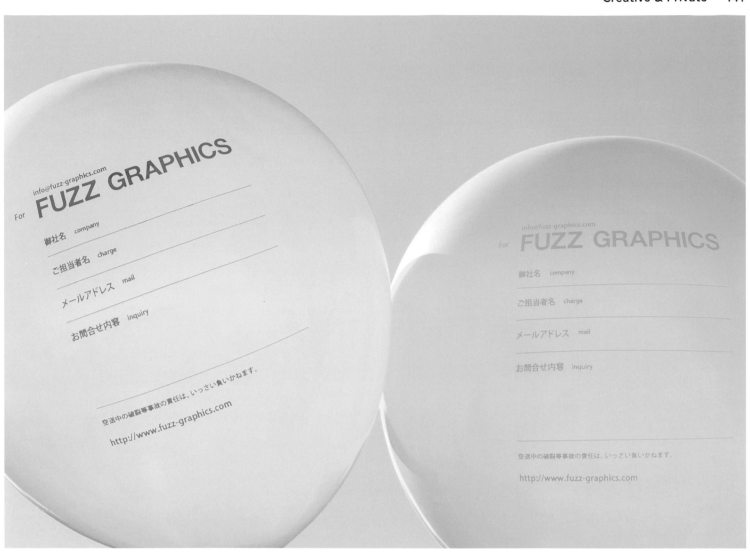

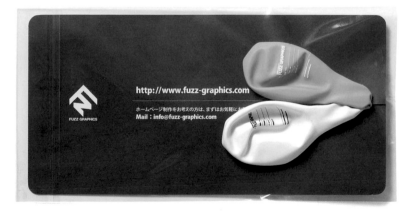

Web の世界からリアルな世界に飛ばした風船付き DM

Web デザインを手がける同社がリアルな世界に向けたアプローチ。風船に名前やメールアドレス、お問い合わせ内容などの記入欄を印刷。『風船に疲れや悩みを吹き込み同社まで飛ばしてください』というメッセージを込めた。

A balloon that takes you from the world of the Web to the real world

An approach to the real world for a company that deals in Web design. The text fields containing names, email addresses and inquiries are printed on the balloon. The message is "Blow your fatigue into the balloon and send it to us."

Web デザイン / 営業用 DM   Web Design / Sales DM

CL, SB：ファズグラフィックス FUZZ GRAPHICS   CD, AD, D：吉川 篤 Atsushi Yoshikawa

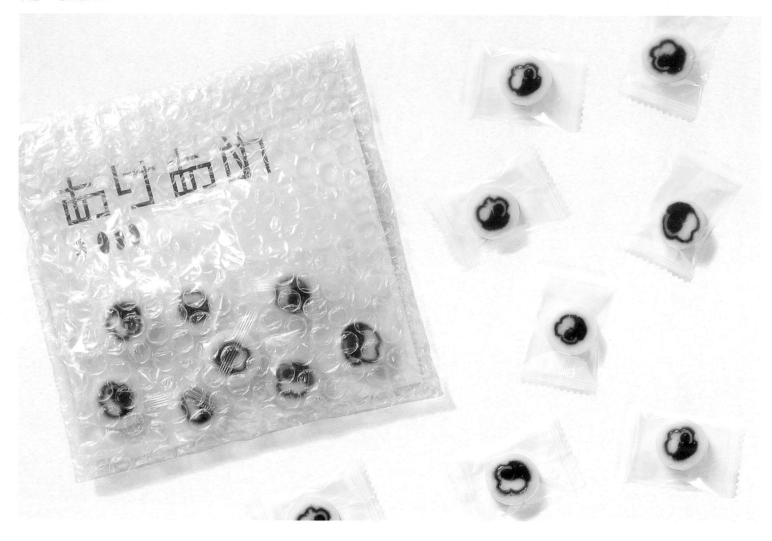

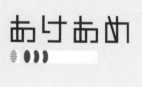

ウェブサイトと連携するオリジナル飴入り年賀状

数ある年賀状の中で埋もれることのないようインパクトの強い形状を考案。『あけおめ』を文字ったタイトルの『あけあめ』にちなみ、オリジナルの金太郎飴を制作。透明のプチプチ袋に入れて送付したことでより印象的なDMとなった。また、あえて年賀状らしい言葉は載せずに自然とウェブサイトへ誘引するように仕掛けたクロスメディア年賀状であることも特徴。

A New Year's card aiming for impact with the words "akeome" (Akemashite omedeto gozaimasu! Happy New Year!)

The aim was a New Year's card that would stand out and not merely be buried under numerous other New Year's cards. It was produced in original Kintaro candy associated with the title of "akeome." So that the candy would not break, it was sent in a bubble-wrap bag, making the DM even more impressive. Also a feature is the fact that a typical New Year's greeting was not included. Instead it contained an invitation to visit the website.

Web制作 / 季節の挨拶状   Web Production / Seasonal Greetings

CL, SB：エレファント・コミュニケーションズ Elephant Communications co., ltd.   AD, D：坂元美奈子 Minako Sakamoto

ウェブサイト　Website

風船ガムで『アイデアを膨らます楽しさ』を体感できるDM

同社が開講するスクールの生徒募集のために制作。『広告はビッグアイデア』をテーマに『よく学び、よくふくらめ。』というコピーを掲げ、自分で噛んで膨らませることができる風船ガムに着目。DM発送と同じタイミングで、大きな風船ガムで浮かび上がる人のポスターや、スペシャルWebサイトを設置するなど展開を行った。

A DM that offers the experience of the "fun of expanding ideas" with bubble-gum

Produced to recruit students for the company's schools. With the theme "Advertising means big ideas," the copy "Study hard and expand your ideas" was used to draw attention to the bubble-gum that can be chewed and then blown into bubbles. A poster featuring a person floating upwards on a large bubble-gum bubble and a special website were developed to time with the dispatch of the DM.

広告代理店 / スクール生募集DM   Advertising Agency / Student Recruitment DM
CL, SB：オグルヴィ・アンド・メイザー・ジャパン Ogilvy & Mather Japan
CD：阿部晶人 Akihito Abe / 橋本孝久 Takahisa Hashimoto   AD：栗塚達也 Tatsuya Kuritsuka /
望月かおり Kaori Mochizuki / 大塚陽子 Yoko Otsuka / 森内憲司 Kenji Moriuchi
CW：中野ほの Hono Nakano / 杉山元規 Motonori Sugiyama

ポスター   Poster

カラーバリエーションが印象深い
展示会の招待状

クリエイター3名の頭文字をとり『フトイ展』と名付けた展示会。
サブタイトルの『LINE』をジッパー加工で表現し、カラフルか
つポップなデザインで仕上げた。

Invitation to an exhibition
with impressive color variations

An exhibition titled Futoi-ten after the first kanji characters in the
three creators' names. For the 2008 exhibition, the subtitle LINE
was expressed with a DM that had undergone a zipper process.

店舗什器、備品、製造、販売 / 展示会の招待状、パンフレット
Manufacturing & Sales of Furniture /
Invitation to an Exhibition, Pamphlet
CL, SB：玉俊工業所　TAMATOSHI Co., LTD.
CD, AD：東 白英　Shirohide Azuma　D：雨谷真理奈　Marina Amagai
DF：ホワイト・ファット・グラフィックス　White Phat Graphics

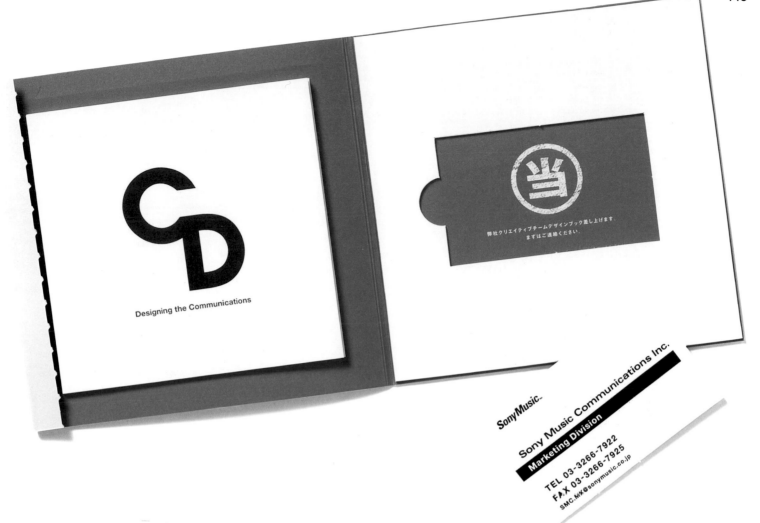

レコードジャケットをモチーフにしたカンパニープレゼン用DM

表全体に銀箔押しやミシン目開封口を施し、受け取った人の興味を惹くとともに、開けてみたいと思ってもらえるDM
を制作。まずコンタクトをいただけるようにと抽選機能を付け、名刺を取り外すと抽選結果が見られるよう仕掛け、ア
タリの方に同社の豪華クリエイティブ集をプレゼントした。

DM for a company presentation with a record jacket motif

The DM was produced with silver foil applied over the entire surface and a perforated opening to arouse the interest of
recipients and entice them to open it. The DM was produced with a lottery function where, when the business card was
removed, the results of the lottery were visible. The winners received a gorgeous creative collection by the company.

デザイン業、広告代理業 / カンパニープレゼンDM　Design, Advertising / Company Presentation
CL, SB：ソニー・ミュージックコミュニケーションズ　Sony music communications Inc.　CD：磯部俊弘　Toshihiro Isobe
AD, D：小島瑞奈　Mizuna Kojima　Planner：伊藤弘康　Hiroyasu Ito　AE：萩原健吾　Kengo Hagiwara

同誌のこだわり『本質を掴む』を『江戸木箸』て表現したDM

100年以上の歴史を持つ手作りの箸『江戸木箸』の『掴む』という行為へのこだわりを同誌のコンセプトと結びつけて表現するとともに、日本特集号の告知であることを強くアピール。縦書きのコピー、そして和紙の風合いを連想させる質感のある紙を使用することでより日本的、かつ味わいのあるDMに仕上げた。

A DM featuring the magazine's "Grasp the essentials" and "Edoki chopsticks"

In addition to connecting the idea of the act of "grasping" Edoki chopsticks that have been made by hand for more than 100 years with the magazine's concepts, the fact that the DM contained notice of a special Japanese edition of the magazine also made a strong appeal. The Japanese copy was written vertically and the paper used had a quality associated with Japanese paper (washi), contributing to the DM's Japanese flavour.

出版 / 広告出稿促進DM　Publishing / Promoting Advertising Sales
CL：ザ・エコノミスト The Economist　CD, Planner：福嶋紳一郎 Shinichiro Fukushima
CD, AD, D：Liyu Min Zie　D：千葉真奈美 Manami Chiba
CW, Planner：髙橋勝也 Katsuya Takahashi　Creative Partner：David Morgan
SB：オグルヴィ・アクション・ジャパン OgilvyAction Japan / オグルヴィ・ワン・ジャパン OgilvyOne Japan

干支にちなんだ言葉遊びが楽しい年賀状

新春の挨拶だけをプリントしたシンプルな年賀状ながら、箔押された筆文字で華やかさを演出。挨拶文の中に交えた干支にちなんだ言葉遊びが目をひく。

A fun New Year's card with wordplay connected to Chinese astrology

A simple New Year's card printed only with the greetings of the season, and a sense of gaiety produced with calligraphic lettering in foil. The wordplay connected to Chinese astrology incorporated into the greeting catches the eye.

人材サービス / 季節の挨拶状　Recruitment Service / Seasonal Greetings
CL：マスメディアン　MASSMEDIAN　AD：池田享史　Takafumi Ikeda　D：高尾元樹　Motoki Takao / 菅 渉宇　Sho Suga /
阿閉高尚　Takahisa Atsuji　CW：藤城敦子　Atsuko Fujishiro　DF, SB：デザインサービス　design service inc.

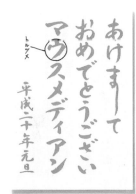

文字を豪華に構成した、
シンプルでインパクトのある移転案内

シンプルで豪華な質感を目指したデザイン事務所の移転案内。箔押しや型押しを施し、紙の質感などのコーディネートにより、アナログな雰囲気を演出した。

A simple yet powerful change of premises notice with a luxurious arrangement of characters

A change of premises notice for a design company where the aim was a simple yet luxurious quality. The notice underwent a foiling and stamping process and an analogue look produced by the quality of the paper etc.

デザイン事務所 / 移転案内　Design Firm / Moving Announcement
CL, DF, SB：アンテナグラフィックベース　Antenna Graphic Base CO., LTD.
AD, D：鷲見 陽　Akira Sumi

モチーフであるゾウに、
干支のイメージを織り込んだ年賀状

社名にちなみ、毎年ゾウをモチーフにした年賀状を制作。形状は同じだが、干支によってデザインに変化をつけている。子年は地にチーズ模様を敷いた。

A New Year's card interwoven with images of Chinese astrology and elephants

In line with the company's name, each year a New Year's card with an elephant motif is produced. The shape remains the same but the design changes according to the Chinese astrology cycle. The Year of the Rat, a cheese pattern was used.

デザイン事務所 / 季節の挨拶状　Design Firm / Seasonal Greetings
CL, DF, SB：エレファントグラフィックス　elephant graphics
D：北野ちあき　Chiaki Kitano

展示テーマである『まきもの』の
イラストを活かしたイベント告知

フェルト作家・濱野由美による、まきものに特化した展示会『まきまきコレクション』の告知DM。作家が描いたイラストを活かして2種のDMを制作。文字に動きをつけることで、まきものの軽やかさも表現した。

Event announcement that incorporates an illustration of a scarf, the theme of the exhibition

A DM giving notice of an exhibition of a scarf collection by felt artist and specialist scarf maker Yumi Hamano. Two versions of the DM were produced using illustrations drawn by the artist herself. Movement was added to the text to express the lightness of the scarves.

フェルト作家 / イベントの告知
Felt Artist / Event Announcement
CL：スポンジ SPONGY　CD, アート：濱野由美 Yumi Hamano
AD, D：野村勝久 Katsuhisa Nomura　D：神 大樹 Taiju Kami
DF, SB：野村デザイン制作室 NOMURA DESIGN FACTORY

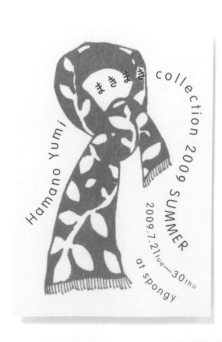

宮田裕美詠

〒939-8081
富山市堀川小泉町657

STRIDE

年賀

温かみと手作り感あふれるうさぎ型の年賀状

受け取った人がおもわず微笑んでしまいそうな、ほんわりとした表情が愛くるしいうさぎ型の年賀状。うさぎの形がくずれないよう1mmの厚紙を使用。温かみと手作り感ある仕上がりとなった。

A New Year's card in the shape of a rabbit full of warmth and a sense of the hand-crafted

A New Year's card in the shape of a rabbit with a face that makes the recipient smile. Cardboard one-millimeter thick was used to prevent the shape of the rabbit collapsing. The result is warm with a sense of the hand crafted.

デザイン事務所 / 季節の挨拶状
Design Firm / Seasonal Greetings
CL, DF, SB：ストライド　STRIDE　AD, D：宮田裕美詠　Yumiyo Miyata

器のイラストをネガ・ポジで表現した
2種類のイベント告知

芸術性と温かみが融合したオリジナリティある陶器を生み出す陶芸作家『Shima ceramica』による『器のかたち展』。作家による器の形のイラストをネガ・ポジで表現し、2種のDMを制作した。

Negative and positive versions of an illustration of a ceramic to produce two types of notice for an event

The Utsuwa no Katachi exhibition by Shima ceramica, a ceramic artist whose work is a unique blend of artistry and warmth. An illustration of the shape of a ceramic vessel made by the artist was expressed in negative and positive versions to produce two types of DM.

陶芸作家 / イベントの告知
Ceramic Artist / Event Announcement
CL, CD：シマセラミカ　Shima ceramica / 晴る　haru
AD, D：野村勝久　Katsuhisa Nomura　D：神 大樹　Taiju Kami
CW：大賀郁子　Ikuko Oga
DF, SB：野村デザイン制作室　NOMURA DESIGN FACTORY

実際に鳥が木にとまっているようにも見える展示会の招待状

若手作家による展覧会『よりどりみどり展』の招待状。作品のイメージを大切にしつつ、ポップな雰囲気と手で触る楽しさも伝えられるよう心がけた。型抜き部分を立ち上げると、実際に鳥が木にとまっているように見えるのも特徴。

An invitation to an exhibition in which a bird appears to be perching on a tree

An invitation to the Yoridori Midori exhibition of work by young artists. The aim was to convey a pop style as well as a tangible sense of fun, while respecting the image of the exhibited works. Features die-cut sections, which when stood up, actually appear to be a bird sitting in a tree.

ギャラリー / 展覧会の招待状
Gallery / Exhibition Invitation
CL：ギャラリー・ストレンガー Gallery Strenger   AD, D：内川たくや Takuya Uchikawa
Project Manager：紙谷岳志 Takeshi Kamiya   DF, SB：東京ピストル TOKYO PISTOL.CO., LTD

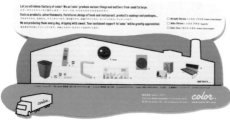

会社を工場に見立てて作品を紹介した、設立一周年の通知DM

様々なカテゴリーでクリエイティブ活動をしているユニットを、ひとつのファクトリー（工場）に見立てて、作品の一部を紹介。会社設立一周年を通知すると同時に、ウェブサイトへの誘引も図った。

DM giving notice of the first anniversary of the founding of the company that likens the company to a factory in presenting its work

The unit that operates in diverse categories of creative activity likened itself to a factory and presented a part of its portfolio. The DM served not only to give notice of the first anniversary of the founding of the company but also to issue an invitation to visit the website.

クリエイティブユニット /
会社設立一周年およびウェブサイトリニューアルの案内
Creative Unit / Information on the First Anniversary of the Founding and Upgrading of the Website
CL, DF, SB：カラー color.inc.   CD, AD：シラスノリユキ
Noriyuki Shirasu   CW：シラスアキコ Akiko Shirasu

クルージングの船を象った
ウェディングパーティーの招待状

船上クルージングパーティーであるため、手描きの船の形に型抜きしたカードを制作。手描きならではの優しさや温もりを意識しつつ、金箔の文字で華やかさもプラスした。

Wedding invitation in the shape of a cruise boat

As the party was to take place on board a boat, the card was produced with a die-cut of the shape of a hand-drawn boat. The design showed an awareness of the softness and warmth that is found with hand-drawn artwork, and extra pizzazz was added with lettering in gold foil.

個人 / ウェディングパーティーの招待状
Personal / Wedding Invitation
CL：渡部基彦 Motohiko Watanabe 加藤晴子 Haruko Kato
AD, D：長澤昌彦 Masahiko Nagasawa
DF, SB：マヒコ Mahiko

航空チケット風にデザインした
ウェディングパーティーの案内状

『新しい出発』をコンセプトに航空チケット風にデザインしたウェディングパーティーの案内状。新郎新婦はもちろん、チケットを受け取った来場者にも新しい出発を運んでくれそうな期待感あふれるDMとなった。

Airline ticket-style design for notice of a wedding reception

Notice of a wedding reception designed in the style of an airline ticket based on the concept of "new departures." The DM creates a sense of anticipation that, not only the bridal couple, but also the guests at the reception who received the ticket will bring a new departure with them.

飲食店 / ウェディングパーティーの案内状
Restaurant / Wedding Invitation
CL：区ト間 kutoma AD：相澤幸彦 Yukihiko Aizawa
D：柏 哲郎 Tetsuro Kashiwa DF, SB：相澤事務所 aizawa office

華やかさとユーモアを演出した
結婚式の招待状

シルク印刷と型抜きを施し、金色を効果的に使いながら、
華やかさとユーモアの詰まった招待状に仕上げた。教会を
象った封筒を制作し、内側にも金色でイラストを描いている。

An invitation to a wedding that displays gaiety and humor

Silkscreen printing, die-cutting and the effective use of the
color gold create a wedding invitation filled with gaiety
and humor. The envelope was produced in the shape of a
church, with gold illustrations drawn on the inner surface.

個人 / 結婚式の招待状
Personal / Wedding Invitation
CL：能谷 剛 Go Noya / 山本敦子 Atsuko Yamamoto
AD：山本ヒロキ Hiroki Yamamoto　DF, SB：マーヴィン MARVIN

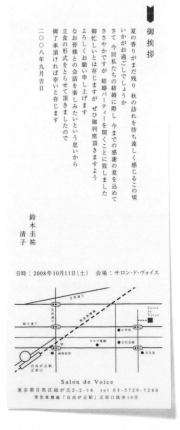

新郎新婦にちなんだウェディングパーティーの案内状

医療関係者同士の結婚のため『寿』のロゴに赤十字を用いて作成。映画好きという
2人の趣味に合わせ、前売り券を意識したデザインにしミシン目加工を施した。ま
たニスの市松文様を用い華やかさを演出した。

Information about a wedding party that incorporates the bridal couple

Produced on the occasion of the marriage of two medical personnel with a
"kotobuki" (congratulations) logo using the Red Cross. In accordance with the movie-
loving couple's hobby, it has been perforated with a design resembling an advance-
sale movie ticket and given extra pizzazz with a varnish in checkered pattern.

個人 / ウェディングパーティーの案内状　Personal / Wedding Invitation
CL：鈴木圭祐、清子 Keisuke, Seiko Suzuki　AD, D：長井健太郎 Kentaro Nagai
DF, SB：グラフレックスディレクションズ　Graflex Directions

NEW
ABSOLUTE
APPEAL:
DIRECT MAIL
DESIGN

CLIENTS クライアント

SUBMITTERS 作品提供社

グラフィックデザイナーのためのWEBディレクション

Pages: 160 (Full Color) ¥5,800 + Tax

昨今、企業や消費者にとって欠かせない媒体となっている WEB。読者が能動的にアクセスするよう、魅せ方が工夫された WEB デザインも増えています。そこで優れたサイトを実例に、「サイトデザインのコツとは？」「WEB で何ができるのか？」を指南するアイデア集を刊行。WEB 関連の仕事が増えつつあるグラフィックデザイナーが、WEB ディレクションする際に必読の 1 冊です。

※ This title is available only in Japan.

世界の名刺「初めまして」のデザイン

Pages: 272 (Full Color) ¥3,800 + Tax

優れた名刺は、印象深い出会いの場をつくり出す一方、名刺の持ち主や組織のアイデンティティーを正確に描写します。本書に収められた 200 以上の作品は、予算とスペースが限られた中で、常に斬新な名刺をつくろうと試行錯誤しているデザイナーたちにとって、インスピレーションあふれる 1 冊になるでしょう。

※ This title is available only in Japan.

@Supermarket: Package Designs
スーパーマーケットデザイン

Pages: 160 (Full Color) ¥7,800 + Tax

生活にまつわるものが全て揃うスーパーマーケットは、デザインの宝庫です。最近は、ブランディングに力を入れたり、オーガニック商品を専門とするような、個性のあるスーパーが増えつつあります。本書は、世界のスーパーマーケットで販売されている、食品や日用品のパッケージ、そしてオリジナルで開発された商品など、暮らしを彩るデザインを紹介します。

This book presents a wide variety of package designs for daily products available at supermarkets –ranging from food & confectionery, beverages to various living products. In addition to package examples of the above categories, this book features "supermarket brand designs".

Eco-Friendly Graphics
エコスタイル グラフィックス

Pages: 224 (Full Color) ¥14,000 + Tax

ここ数年、多くの企業は「環境」「健康」をテーマに商品開発や広告コミュニケーションをすることを主流としています。今やこれらのテーマは企業存続に欠かせません。地球にやさしい、人にやさしい、体にやさしいというテーマは、今後も多くの企業にとって、大きなキーワードとなっていくことでしょう。本書はこれらをテーマとした商品広告から企業広告までを紹介します。

This title introduces the good examples of the advertising campaigns based on the concept of eco-friendly. The selected advertisements for foods, electric appliances, beauty products and services are elaborately presented from this highly respected point of view, "eco-friendly." This is the second edition of "Earth-Friendly Graphics"

Smart Designs: Business Cards
世界の名刺 ベストアイデアブック

Pages: 232 (Full Color) ¥3,800 + Tax

出会った最初に交わす「ごあいさつのツール」である名刺。ちょっとした工夫を加えるだけで、取引先との会話がはずみ、相手に、好印象を残すことができるのです。本書では、デザイナーやクリエイターのみならず多岐にわたる企業の秀逸なデザインやコンセプトの作品を集めました。ビジネスチャンスを広げる、効果的な名刺作成のアイデアが満載です！

Business cards serve as indispensable communication tools in many countries around the world. The featured works represent a wide range of businesses including restaurant owners, car dealers, graphic designers, photographers, stylists, copywriters, DJs and more.

Take One For Free !
「ご自由にお持ちください」のデザイン

Pages: 192 (Full Color) ¥9,800 + Tax

店頭に置かれるパンフレット・リーフレット、街なかで配られるサンプル、専用ラックに設置されているフリーペーパー…etc. 今、誰もが自由に持ち帰ることができる広告物は、身近にあふれています。だからこそ、消費者が思わず手にとり、心を掴むような工夫が必要です。本書は「タダでもらえる」をキーワードに、デザイン的に優れ、アイディアにあふれた広告物を業種別に幅広く紹介します。

As you just walk around the city or at the stores, you have often found dozens of advertising materials are free to take away, such as pamphlets, leaflets, samples, catalogs and etc. With "Take One for Free" as the keyword, this book shows a variety of such outstanding works attracting the target customers

Contemporary Japanesque Design
モダンジャパンスタイルデザイン

Page: 224 (Full Color) ¥14,000 + Tax

伝統の "和" を巧みに現代風にアレンジした "和モダン" のデザイン。近年、クリエイティブ業界で一つのジャンルとして確立しつつあり、作品が次々と生まれています。 本書では、見る人の心をつかみ新しい感覚を抱かせる最新のポスター・パッケージ・プロダクトなどを多数紹介します。さらに「キャッチコピー」のカテゴリを加えた、バラエティ豊かな一冊です。

Breaking away from traditional Japanese-style designs, "contemporary Japanese-style design" has established itself as a genre in the creative world. This is the third edition to "Neo Japanesque Graphics" and "Neo Japanesque Design" and introduces the newest design works in advertising, packaging, products, shop image, shop tools, logos and etc.

Girl, Illustrated:
Japanese Manga, Anime, and Video Game Characters
ガールズグラフ

Page: 208 (192 in Color) ¥2,800 + Tax

日本が世界に誇る「オタク市場」。それをリードするクリエイター約 100 人の仕事を紹介した「コミック・アニメ・ゲーム・ライトノベル系のイラストレーターファイル」ができました。コミック編集者・ゲームプロデューサーをはじめ、広告制作者や出版関係者、キャラクタービジネス関係者などの情報源として活用できる貴重な 1 冊です。

Manga, Anime, and games are the culture that Japan can boast to the world. This is a file of about 100 professional illustrators who rise above the crowd in the world of such cultures. It deals with about 500 high quality works with the taste of manga and anime which have been getting popular for more wide range of people in all over the world.

装飾活字
アンティークフレーム＆パーツ素材集（CD-ROM 付）

Page: 160 (Full Color)　￥7,800 + Tax

1185

装飾活字とは、活版印刷時代に作られた草花の図案を象った活字のことで、古くは 15 世紀から、ヨーロッパの書物や印刷物を美しく彩ってきました。はんこのような活字を１つ１つ組み合わせて印刷するという当時の印刷技術の特徴から、上下左右のどの組み合わせで組んでも美しいデザインになるように作られています。この特性をそのまま生かし、高品質なデジタル素材としてデータ化しました。今までにないクオリティを実現し、プロ・アマチュアを問わず、幅広いニーズに応えます。

※ This title is available only in Japan.

New Girly Graphics
ニューガーリーグラフィックス

Page: 200 (Full Color)　￥9,800 + Tax

1190

昨今、「ガーリーなファッション」「ガーリーな雑誌」「ガーリーなメイク」…といった言葉の使われ方をするように、視覚イメージにおいても、ガーリーテイストはひとつの形容詞のような役割を果たすようになりました。広告・パッケージ・エディトリアル・プロダクトなど、あらゆる領域で「ガーリー」な世界が表現されたグラフィック作品を、コンテンツごとに紹介します。

The girly image has been having unfailing power with great impact these days, which attract a broad range of audience. This is the second edition of one of our strongest titles "Girly Graphics", featuring current advertisements, catalogues, posters, shop cards, direct mail, and more. The works will be classified by the image words such as "Glamorous & Poisonous", "Pure & Natural", "Cute & Rock'n'Roll" and "Romantic & Fairy tale"

Graphic Explanation in Advertisement
広告の中の図説デザイン

Page: 176 (Full Color)　￥9,800 + Tax

1206

商品の機能や使い方を説明する時、サービスの特徴や仕組みを簡潔に伝えたい時、様々な側面で「図説」は効果的な手法となります。そこで本書では、ポイントや情報を整理し、意図を分かりやすく伝えている「図説」を一堂に集めました。さまざまな広告物の中で使われている機能性・デザイン性に富んだ説明図の数々を、細部までクローズアップして紹介します。

When you explain the function and the use of the products, "graphic explanation" is a very useful tool. This book shows excellent samples of "graphic explanation" which organize the information and the points successfully to make them easily understood.
Many kinds of well-designed and functional graphic explanation of various advertisements are introduced categorized by industries.

カタログ・新刊のご案内について
総合カタログ、新刊案内をご希望の方は、下記パイ インターナショナルへご連絡下さい。

パイ インターナショナル
TEL：03-3944-3981　FAX：03-5395-4830
e-mail：sales@pie-intl.com

CATALOGS and INFORMATION ON NEW PUBLICATIONS
If you would like to receive a free copy of our general catalog
or details of our new publications, please contact PIE International Inc.

PIE International Inc.
FAX +81-3-5395-4830
e-mail: sales@pie-intl.com

ターゲットに効く！　DMデザイン
New Absolute Appeal : Direct Mail Design

2010 年 2 月 7 日　初版第 1 刷発行

Art Directior & Cover Designer
松村大輔　Daisuke Matsumura

Designer
公平恵美　Emi Kohei

Photographer
藤本邦治　Kuniharu Fujimoto

Writer
久保田裕子　Yuko Kubota
小間浩子　Hiroko Koma

Translator
三木アソシエイツ　Miki Associates

Editor
宮崎亜美　Ami Miyazaki
森山晋平　Shinpei Moriyama

発行元　パイ インターナショナル
〒 114-0024　東京都北区西ヶ原 4-3-6（東京支社）
TEL：03-3944-3981　FAX：03-5395-4830
sales@pie-intl.com
〒 335-0001　埼玉県蕨市北町 1-19-21-301（本社）

印刷・製本　株式会社サンニチ印刷
制作協力　PIE BOOKS

ISBN978-4-7562-4016-3 C3070

Printed in Japan

内容に関するお問い合わせは下記までご連絡ください。
PIE BOOKS　TEL：03-5395-4819